SpringerBriefs in Accounting

Series editors

More information about this series at http://www.springer.com/series/11900

Epameinondas Katsikas · Francesca Manes Rossi
Rebecca L. Orelli

Towards Integrated Reporting

Accounting Change in the Public Sector

Springer

Epameinondas Katsikas
Kent Business School
University of Kent
Kent
UK

Rebecca L. Orelli
Department of Management
University of Bologna
Bologna
Italy

Francesca Manes Rossi
Management and Innovation Systems
University of Salerno
Fisciano
Italy

ISSN 2196-7873 ISSN 2196-7881 (electronic)
SpringerBriefs in Accounting
ISBN 978-3-319-47234-8 ISBN 978-3-319-47235-5 (eBook)
DOI 10.1007/978-3-319-47235-5

Library of Congress Control Number: 2016954516

Printed on acid-free paper

This Springer imprint is published by Springer Nature
The registered company is Springer International Publishing AG
The registered company address is: Gewerbestrasse 11, 6330 Cham, Switzerland

Foreword

Integrated Reporting and the Public Domain—Engagement with Practice

Accounting and management research is often conceived as applied research in that the focus of study is made up of technologies and technical practices used by practitioners in social and organisational settings. This stands in marked contrast to the physical sciences, where the focus of study is mainly physical matter. At the international level, research is generally a requirement for academic career progression and an important contributor to the development of knowledge and scholarship (Evans et al. 2011).

The impact of research on some disciplines is easy for the lay person to comprehend. For example, in medicine, advances in medical procedures and development of new drugs may result in clear benefits to society. For accounting, this impact is not so easy to discern. For instance, in the field of accounting, there have been claims that research has become too far removed from the interests of the professionals and practitioners. Researchers in turn point to the shortcomings of current professional practices. Indeed, some in the accounting research community go so far as to consider that many practical issues of concern to professional accountants do not warrant the attention of researchers (Evans et al. 2010).

I am pleased to highlight that the authors of this book have successfully bridged the gap between academic work and practice. This book is a prime illustration of how academic work can inform emerging practices—in this case, integrated reporting (IR).

IR is emerging as a strategic communication tool to integrate different perspectives on value creation, offering new insights on organisations' approaches to sustainability, corporate governance, natural capital, intellectual capital, human capital and social capital. To date, there have been many studies into models to be adopted and theoretical perspectives that examine the motivation behind the introduction of IR with regard to private entities (Bernardi et al. 2016). However, there is a lack of research about the suitability of IR to satisfy the needs of the public domain.

What has emerged in practice, and has been highlighted by scholars, is that IR makes sense only if it is the result of "integrated thinking" developed inside the organisation—without integrated thinking the process of IR may be little more than a marketing activity. The authors point out in this present book that the adoption of IR should result in a management accounting change within the organisation, and the related disclosures should be considered as the final step that flourishes from an institutionalisation process of integrated thinking inside the organisation.

The authors raise the question: Is IR suitable for public sector entities or is it too ambitious to concentrate all financial and non-financial information related to a public entity in one report?

This book provides insights into why and how a public organisation should deal with IR. The path for the institutionalisation of IR in the public sector is complex and cannot be taken for granted. The book aims to shed light on the process, unravelling themes both theoretically, adopting the lens of accounting change, and empirically, by discussing an in-depth case of a state-owned enterprise's adoption of integrated thinking.

The book has four chapters to guide the reader to an understanding of the process underpinning the adoption of integrated thinking and IR. In Chap. 1, the authors explore the relationship between context and public sector organisations, highlighting the pivotal role of these kinds of entities in addressing sustainability. The creation of "public value" for the benefit of both present and future generations requires an integrated approach to the management of all the capitals, while ensuring sustainable development. There is in-depth discussion as to why IR and integrated thinking may represent a new frontier for public sector organisations.

In Chap. 2, the authors offer a theoretical lens to explore different approaches to strategic thinking. For this reason, various institutional theory strands complementary with management theories highlight the role of routines, and the possible changes necessary to internalise integrated thinking are discussed.

Chapter 3 provides various steps to the development of an IR framework. For this reason, other communication tools usually adopted by both private and public organisations are discussed—namely, the annual report, corporate governance report, corporate social responsibility report and intellectual capital report. Furthermore, both the South African Integrated Reporting Framework and International <IR> Framework are illustrated, providing several reflections on challenges offered by the adoption of IR.

Chapter 4 offers an understanding of the processes characterising the adoption of integrated thinking. To this end, the Hera Group case study provides useful "lessons to learn." The case study analysis not only considers external change, integrated thinking and IR disclosures prepared by this public sector entity, but also examines changes over time, as well as internal changes, which can be viewed as the progressive internalisation of integrated thinking.

The book will be of benefit to academics, practitioners, consultants and policy makers as well as students interested in the adoption of IR. Additionally, it provides insights into the reasons for public organisations entering into integrated thinking while developing a stakeholder engagement approach in formulating their long-term strategies. The book is well grounded in theory and therefore useful in masters' courses discussing accountability in public organisations, sustainability issues and stakeholder engagement in public entities.

James Guthrie
Distinguished Professor of Accounting
Department of Accounting
and Corporate Governance
Macquarie University, Australia

References

Dumay J, Bernardi C, Guthrie J, Demartini P (2016) Integrated reporting: a literature review of an emerging research field. Acc Forum 40(3):166–185.

Evans E, Burritt R, Guthrie J (eds) (2010) Accounting education at a crossroad in 2010. Academic Leadership Series, vol 1. The Institute of Chartered Accountants in Australia and the Centre for Accounting, Governance and Sustainability.

Evans E, Burritt R, Guthrie J (eds) (2011) Bridging the gap between academic accounting research and professional practice. Academic Leadership Series, vol 2. The Institute of Chartered Accountants in Australia and the Centre for Accounting, Governance and Sustainability.

Contents

Chapter 1
Setting the Context for Integrated Reporting in the Public Sector

Abstract The central aim of this chapter is to discuss why Integrated Reporting can represent a new frontier for public sector accounting studies. From this perspective, the chapter introduces the reader to the relationships between environmental and sustainability issues and public sector organizations. These points of view have been considered pivotal for an in depth understanding of the value creation process in the public domain. However, to properly understand how public value is created, the role of intangibles must also be considered. The above mentioned reasons pave the way for the adoption of integrated reporting not only as a communication tools but, above all, as a strategic tool which can open the opportunity to experiment with management change. The chapter ends by identifying the contents to be discussed in the following chapters.

Keywords Integrated reporting · Public sector · Intangibles · Social responsibility · Value creation · Management accounting change

1.1 The Scenario: Integrated Reporting and the Public Sector

Public administration has been involved over the last decades in a profound process of change in management, organization and information systems, in order to provide both more efficient allocation of public resources and accomplish a claim for better public performances. This movement, well-known as New Public Management (Aucoin 1990; Hood 1991; Thomas 2012) has given rise to a further process of change, labelled as New Public Governance, basically intended to make public administration more sensitive to citizens needs and to ensure greater trans-

---

This chapter was written by Francesca Manes Rossi.

E. Katsikas et al., *Towards Integrated Reporting*,
SpringerBriefs in Accounting, DOI 10.1007/978-3-319-47235-5_1

parency and flexibility, supporting citizen engagement in political life (Bovaird 2005; Pollitt and Bouckaert 2011; Osborne et al. 2014). Thus, a growing interest in how public sector organizations are managed, how they perform and how an impact takes place on the external environment has spread out worldwide.

Beyond traditional accounting tools suitable to provide an overview of the financial situation of the entity, a high attention has been progressively devoted to consider to what extent a public sector entity operates coherently with its own mission. To this end, new accounting technologies related to performance measurement and management have been widely adopted in the aim of keeping under control outputs, efficiency, cost saving and productivity (Broadbent and Guthrie 1992; Guthrie et al. 1999; Hoque and Moll 2001). The attention paid to budgeting, spending, and managing public money has increased enormously, and new public financial management (NPFM) systems have been considered essential for effective and sustainable economic management and public service delivery (Olson et al. 1998; Guthrie et al. 1999, 2005).

At the same time, a large number of initiatives have emerged in the last decades promoting voluntary sustainability reporting in the public sector (e.g. CIPFA 2005; GRI 2005; United Nations 2008; World Bank 2008). The European Commission has also strongly encouraged central and local government to adopt sustainability reporting.

Scholars are paying growing attention to the flourishing different kinds of sustainability and environmental reporting, claiming the leading role of public sector organizations in a more sustainable future and the related relevance of sustainability accounting and accountability (Ball et al. 2014; Dumay et al. 2010; Guthrie and Farneti 2008; Olson et al. 1998; Mussari and Monfardini 2010). Other scholars have highlighted the possible role of these types of reports as a means to gain legitimacy (Deegan et al. 2002).

Despite the informative power of all these new forms of reporting, information on sustainability issues are not able to completely satisfy the accountability needs for different types of stakeholders. Beside financial and sustainability reports, citizens would be possibly interested in discovering more about present and future services delivered by public entities, being the citizen not just users but also *co-producers* of the service (Osborne et al. 2013). More information that should be addressed using accounting tools are those relating to future strategies and plans, alliances and partnerships, networking activities, governance mechanisms in place, all combined with forms of citizens' engagement. Accounting, in fact, is not limited to calculation and metrics—even if this information is fundamental throughout social practice—but also brings about ideas which produce a mediating attitude to link actors with a common narrative (Miller and Power 2013).

However, the risk of information overload should be considered. As scholars have already noticed, too much information can turn in a flood of misinformation (Grimmelikhuijsen et al. 2013), reducing, rather than increasing the interest of citizens in reporting provided by public entities. To avoid this risk, information provided should be concise, understandable for citizens with no specific competences in accounting matters, should explain not only what a public organization has already done but also future plans, clarifying financial sustainably while addressing intergenerational equity. Moreover, governance mechanisms should be presented and the business models could be rendered to all different stakeholders. In particular, all this information should not be presented separately, and the connectivity between them should be clearly shown, following an integrated approach.

Scholars have already debated about the suitability of existing forms of reporting in public sector entities in order to give adequate answers relating to the information needs of different categories of stakeholders (Mack and Ryan 2007; Arnaboldi and Lapsley 2009; Walker 2009; Cohen and Karatzimas 2015).

What has progressively emerged is that the modern economic environment asks for information that goes beyond not only the traditional financial reporting, but even the sustainability reporting, giving adequate room to future plans and developments (Fasan 2013) and that this information should be concise, easy to understand and—of course—fair (Cohen and Karatzimas 2015).

Under this wave, a new tool is gaining importance and receiving attention both by standard setters and scholars, both in the private and public domain of Integrated Reporting (IR).

This tool is certainly born in the private domain, resulting from the need to systematize different kinds of information in one report (Abeysekera 2013; Busco et al. 2013; Druckman and Fries 2010; Eccles and Krzus 2010; Eccles and Serafeim 2014; Jensen and Berg 2012) and it has spread quickly, especially in South Africa, receiving the first regulation, along with the Anglo-Saxon countries (Robertson and Samy 2015; Rowbottom and Locke 2016). Rooted in the idea of the triple bottom line reporting of financial, social and environmental activities, the IR can provide information on the different types of tangible and intangible resources involved in the value creation process within the organization.

What has emerged in practice and has been highlighted by scholars is that Integrated Reporting makes sense only if the result is of an "integrated thinking" developed inside the organization, otherwise this tool would possibly be reduced to merely a marketing tool (Adams 2015; Higgins et al. 2014). The point of reference adopted in developing the present book, is that the adoption of IR is the result of a management accounting change within the organization and the related disclosure should be considered as the final step that flourishes from the progressive institutionalization process inside the organization of integrated thinking (Higgins et al. 2014).

One question that may arise could be: is the IR suitable for public sector entities or it is too ambitious to concentrate all financial and non-financial information related to a public entity in one report?

The chapter intends to give an answer to this question, by analysing if the constituent elements of integrated reporting can be considered as a point of reference for public entities.

1.2 The Relationship: Public Sector and Environment

While discussing the relationship between public sector organization and the environment, a first step necessary to frame the discussion is to define what can be included in the concept of the public sector. In accordance with Broadbent and Guthrie (1992, p. 3) "the public sector is that part of a nation's economic activity which is traditionally owned and controlled by government… the public sector is composed of those public organizations which provide utilities and services to the community which have traditionally been seen as essential to the fabric of our society". Thus the boundaries of the public sector are extremely wide and sometimes blurred, including also public corporations operating in the market, as well as listed state-owned enterprises (Ball et al. 2014). Despite the material differences in the nature of activities performed by this complex and heterogeneous set of organization, all of them have at their core ethical values and the public interest as a common denominator.

Moreover, New Public Management has progressively introduced logics, metrics and management tools traditionally developed in the private domain (Broadbent and Guthrie 1992; Hood 1995; Pollitt and Bouchaert 2011). However, while the ultimate goal in private entities will be a financial gain, even respecting the environment, public entities should be basically interested in providing goods and services in accordance with citizens' needs and environment protection should be part of their policy in order to ensure intergenerational equity. Public sector entities are responsible towards the community not only for resources absorbed in the production process but also for re-generating and/or protecting natural resources. It is worthy to highlight that public governments also play a relevant role in stimulating corporate social responsibility (CSR) behaviour by private entities, through regulation, requirement and policies (Steurer 2010), but this issue will not be discussed in the current research.

The consideration of environmental and sustainability issues by public sector organizations has been considered as essential to the fabric of our society (Ball et al. 2014) and distinct in the concept of CSR related to profit-oriented entities (Friedman 1970). As noted by Broadbent and Guthrie (1992), in the public domain there are different groups of entities that can be identified by looking at the different strengths of ownership and control. Some of these entities are closer to the market than others, thus accounting tools can play a different role in respect to decision making, control or accountability.

The conceptualization of sustainability in the public sector is holistic, being devoted to include action already taken, but also the gap that needs to be overcome in order to improve environmental and sustainability conditions in regard to financial and social aspects. As Birney et al. state, "*Public sector organisations are central to the delivery of sustainable development. Every aspect of their role—from education to environmental services, and from planning to social care—shapes how people live their lives*" (2010: 3).

Other environmental issues that public entities should consider are related to climate change and the progressive depletion of natural resources. This type of issue calls for active actions to be undertaken by public organizations in their activities, but also as watchdogs, promoting close attention by private entities. In this regard, governments, both at national and local level, may adopt different kinds of policies. The adoption of accounting tools supporting both management and communication process of policies undertaken towards a higher social responsibility should be both related to internal factors, namely to the governance of human resources, and to the external factors (GRI 2005). Moreover, the adoption of policy addressing the social responsibility can be implicit or explicit (Matten and Moon 2008). In this sense, providing a vehicle for communicating how vague political objectives relating to environment and sustainability, have been translated into programs and actions, and would offer a better understanding of how an entity deals with its core mission. Discussing sustainability reporting, Gray (2006) has identified three different approaches: under the *managerialist approach* data is reported assuming that no conflict exists between the traditional economic criteria and social and environmental aspects, thus providing only selected data. The *triple bottom line approach* equates economic, social and environmental activities of the organization, thus considering the consequences of corporate behavior and possibly the structures and governance of the organization. The third approach, labelled as *ecologically- and eco-justice-informed approach*, is built around the notion of ecological footprints and social justice, so it requires one to identify if an organization is socially and environmentally sustainable. The condition of un-sustainability should draw radical revision on how economic organizations are managed. The three approaches differ in their contributions to value-creation and to organizational performance, as discussed in the following paragraph.

Gray's work (2006) has opened a new approach to sustainability reporting: as Dumay et al. (2010) underline, a new perspective should be embraced, considering how unsustainable the organizations are. In proposing this question, public organizations have to face a different range of personal, social and environmental cost. In fact, most public organizations cannot rely on economic outcomes. Moreover, as Dumay et al. clearly state, sustainability is not a managerialism measurement exercise, but "what is required is action, not measurement and reporting" (Dumay et al. 2010: 542). Thus a change should start from inside the organization, involving managers and employers as well as other stakeholders connected to the process of value-creation, in the pursuit of sustainability.

In some countries, such as the UK and New Zealand have had various sustainability initiatives put in place to protect the environment, both at national and at local level (Lewis 2000; Ball et al. 2014).

On the basis of the abovementioned reasons, frameworks on sustainability accounting specifically devoted to public sector organization have emerged in only a decade. In 2005 the Global Reporting Initiative issued the Public Agencies Sector supplement to its reporting framework (GRI 2005). One year after the Chartered Institute of Public Finance and Accountancy proposed a framework for public sector entities sustainability reporting (CIPFA 2006). In 2010 the Association of

Chartered Certified Accountants prepared a report (ACCA 2010) summarizing all guidelines issued on the matter and, above all discussing the role of public sector sustainability reporting. More specifically, the ACCA report underlines the need to take into account the particular responsibility and motivation that governments and public sector entities face.

1.3 The Missing Link: Intangibles, Social Responsibility and Value Creation

Discussing the relevance of the relation between public sector and the environment, the relevance of internal resources was briefly presented, in particular the relevance of providing a clear and sound governance of human resources. In the present section the discussion is enlarged including all intangibles resources that are considered essential to the value creation process as well as to the relationship between intangibles and social responsibility.

1.3.1 The Role of Intangibles

It is a matter of fact that radical changes occurred in the use of assets by organizations; in the so-called knowledge economy, there has been a structural turn from the prevalent use of tangible assets characterising the industrial economy, to the prevalent use of intangible assets in the new economy. In this new kind of productive system, production of goods and services is strongly characterized by the use of assets that are not only intangible, but also not completely controlled by the organization or being a legal right of property which is not identifiable (Lev et al. 2005). Innovation became the key to success in the business world and assets like research and development, brand, creativity, as well as innovative procedures, human resources are essential in a competitive environment. Nahapiet and Ghoshal (1998) have discusses the so-called "organizational advantage" referring to the capabilities of organizations in creating and sharing knowledge, which includes both the organizational principles by which human resource are coordinated and communicated, along with tacit knowledge (Edvisson and Malone 1997). Since the end of the '90 the discussion around so called intellectual capital (IC) has attracted the attention of accounting scholars, which have discussed the management, measurement and disclosure of intangibles (Bontis 1998; Guthrie 2001; Petty and Guthrie 2000). While in the traditional industrial economy cost-focused reporting methods used to provide an adequate picture of firm performance, nowadays there is the issue of disclosing the value of intangibles (Lev et al. 2005). The fundamental problem perceived by scholars is related to the recognition of these types of assets, as they often do not meet the required accounting definition, making it difficult to

Fig. 1.1 The role of intangible in the S&P 500 Market Value

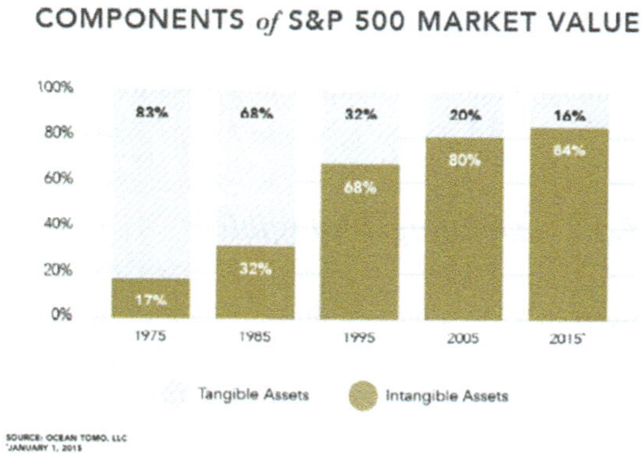

fully recognize their value through traditional accounting tools, thus excluding them from financial statement (Wayne 2001). Several models have been created to measure the IC (Bontis 2001), but their full recognition in the traditional financial report nonetheless remains to be achieved. Notwithstanding, their contribution to the long-term generating ability of the organization is undeniable (Robb et al. 2001) and some research has been undertaken to demonstrate the relationship between intellectual capital and firms' market value and financial performance (Chen et al. 2005; Maditinos et al. 2011). Every year Ocean Tomo, an Intellectual Capital Merchant Banc which provides management and advisory services centred on IC, releases a study dedicated to intangible asset value of the S&P 500. The last study available refers to 2015 and shows a terrific inversion of percentage between tangible and intangible assets, as the Fig. 1.1 clarify.

In the public sector domain there is a growing interest by scholars (synthesis presented by Dumay et al. 2015; Ferenhof et al. 2015; Guthrie and Dumay 2015) even if empirical research is still lacking in numbers. However, in public organizations the recognition and communication of intangible assets is pivotal, being their actions' effectiveness scarcely measurable by traditional accounting tools and having relevant inputs (e.g. skills, competences, routine and procedures, information systems) and outputs (public welfare, quality of life, protection of the environment, social capital) intangible in their nature. Indeed, financial resources are merely an instrument rather than an end to a means for a large part of these organizations (Del Bello 2006; Ramírez 2010; Manes-Rossi et al. 2016).

Moreover, as noticed by Guthrie and Dumay (2015), the public sector continues to face constant changes in production and service delivery, new technology is setting new challenges and there is an increasing need to understand how knowledge through IC can be supportive. A recent literature review by Dumay et al. (2015) highlights that research in the public sector domain so far focuses on central government and central government agencies and education (basically universities), in Europe (especially Italy and Spain). Empirical research using case studies are mainly devoted to IC management control and strategy. Consequently, it appears to be clear that more than in the past, two different but converging sets of research are worthy of being developed: the first to clarify how managing knowledge through IC would support in creating public value in public organizations, the second to identify suitable techniques and tools to truly capture the value of the entity.

1.3.2 Defining Intangibles

Even if IC is a unitary phenomenon (Zambon 2004) an effort to identify the different types of intangible resources would be beneficial for a better understanding and management. Thus, a prodromal step back in this research is an identified component of IC, being a lack of consensus on their possible definitions, in order to clarify what is included under this "umbrella" term. A comprehensive understanding of the intangibles and IC component from an accounting perspective can begin with the definition of intangibles provided by the International Public Sector Accounting Standard Boards (IPSASB) which have issued the International Public Sector Accounting Standard (IPSAS) 31, drawn primarily from International Accounting Standard (IAS) 38, Intangible Assets published by the International Accounting Standards Board (IASB). Both standards define intangible assets as "an identifiable non-monetary asset without physical substance". The characteristics that allow us to recognize an intangible as an asset to be included in the financial statement are: *identifiability*, *control over a resource* and *existence of future economic benefits* or service potential.

However, as Cañibano et al. (2000) suggests, the accounting description of assets is not completely able to fully describe the notion of intangible values because it excludes several components (reputation, organizational knowledge, loyalty etc.) which do not meet the prescribed characteristics. Thus, while legal right (like concessions, trademarks, copyrights etc.) can be easily identified and recognized in financial reporting due to the existence of a legally binding contract to enforce the right, there are other kinds of intangibles which cannot be safeguarded by a law or a contractual agreement. Grüber (2014) divides these other items into *economic values*, which are knowledge that can be used by the organization in a not exclusive manner (like trade secrets, know-how some software applications etc.) and *economic advantages*, which refer to those elements that cannot be recognized separately nor measured individually (e.g. R&D expenses, corporate culture, advertising and reputation, relationships with suppliers).

A different approach, which Grüber (2014) names as *economic classifications scheme*, is rooted in the economic value of intangibles considering the role that different elements can play in the value creation process in the specific organization. Making reference to the accounting standard setter, it worth noting that the IASB in IFRS 3 for business combination, distinguishes marketing-related, customer-related, artistic-related, contract-based as well as technology-based assets (IFRS 3 par.IE16). However, also in this standard, the IASB does not include those assets that cannot be clearly identified.

The classification upon which most scholars agree, also in the public domain, identifies *human capital*, *structural* (or internal or organizational) *capital* and *relational* (or external) *capital* (Guthrie 2001; Meritum 2002; Serrano Cinca et al. 2003; Bronzetti and Sicoli 2011; Cohen and Vlismas 2013; Secundo et al. 2015). The three categories are briefly discussed hereafter, and much literature is developing in regard to public organizations, which would deserve a separate investigation.

1.3.2.1 Human Capital

Lev in his research (2001) attributes to human capital, the large increases in the market value of firms between 1980s and 1990s. Undoubtedly skilled staff can lead to future economic benefits and in having such skilled staff, organizations (private or public) should invest in training. This type of talent requires a proper management increase, in terms of knowledge and experience which should remain inside the organization. Thus, ad hoc programs to develop the workforce through both theoretical and "on the job" training, have to be adopted, therefore promoting commitment, lower turnover, internal information systems to enable sharing which encourage that information is used extensively across different functions (Drucker 1994).

At the same time, employees are required to invest their own "intangible resources" in the same organization in order to show growth. Of course employees will be willing to invest energy in the extent that they see the opportunity to benefit in terms of remuneration, career perspectives, non-financial recognition and personal fulfillment. The organization has to face some concerns in relation to investment in human capital, such as the possibility of having a crucial resource leaving the company, or poor cooperation and consequently a limited spread of competences across different functions, or the failure to create a culture of change and innovation. Recent research in the public sector has demonstrated the positive relationship of employee capability and satisfaction on the value creation process (Massingham and Tam 2015).

1.3.2.2 Structural Capital

Structural capital (often identified also as organizational or internal capital) correlates to the set of skills and knowledge that have been institutionalized inside the organizational processes, routines and culture (Edvinsson and Malone 1997; Meritum 2002; Ramírez 2010).

Concrete examples of structural capital have been identified by scholars as culture, reputation, flexibility, infrastructure, such as IT systems, the organizational structure, processes and procedures (Grüber 2014).

Investment in structural capital is crucial to enable and facilitate the diffusion and sharing of knowledge, a reduction in the time needed for technical activities and lastly to increase employee's productivity.

Of course investment in infrastructure (e.g. ITC) would not give any positive impact on value creation per se, only if correlated to other complementary investments in human capital, for instance education, training and motivation. Once again, structural capital is strictly related to accounting information systems and internal control mechanisms and should promote innovation inside the organization. For this reason, investing in this component of IC should lead to obtaining a positive impact on value creation.

1.3.2.3 Relational Capital

Relational capital (or external capital) indicates the relationships that an organization has with external stakeholders, such as suppliers, customers or investors. In public organizations investment in this kind of capital can seem at a first glance less obvious. However, as highlighted by Bronzetti and Sicoli (2011: 87) "improvement in relations with the recipients of public activities (users of services) and, more generally, with social partners, facilitates public service workers' understanding and, therefore, ability to meet the needs of the community". The growth of this component of IC is beneficial in order for a public organization to increase its legitimacy and enhance accountability.

The question at this stage is—to what extent intangibles resources (alias intellectual capital) can contribute to enhance the value creation process?

The powerful metaphor adopted by several authors (Edvinsson and Malone 1997; Andriessen 2004) to emphasize the role of intangible assets, compares organization to a tree where fruit and leaves can be considered as the output, the trunk and branches can be associated with the structure of the organization which, together with the fruit and leaves represent how the organization is known in its environment and intangibles are identified as the roots, which are of course essential for the flourishing of the tree. In this approach, Edvisson's (2002) main concern is the growth of human capital. Managers of course need the support of the accounting systems, because it is essential to know what forces create value. However, they also necessitate new perspectives on how the organization works. Thus, a report for internal purposes for measuring the IC is required. Of course an external report on IC is also a requirement in order to reduce information asymmetry between investors (or more generally lenders) and the organization. The typical tool to disclose IC has been considered indicators. However, as Mouritsen et al. (2001) points out, onside stories and sketches deserve to be disclosed: "Indicators create seriousness because they are published. Stories create comprehensiveness of the strategy proposed although it cannot be defined in its details. Sketches, which visualize the relationship the story, produce and suggest the connectivity in the indicators reported" (Mouritsen et al. 2001: 418). This approach would not allow showing a precise evaluation of IC, rather to describe the way value is created.

1.3.3 The Link Between Intangibles and Social Responsibility

Having discussed the role of intangibles, as well as the role of social responsibility, the missing link between them needs to be unveiled, in the aim of discovering how managing intangibles would increase the sustainability of the public organization, through the value creation process.

In fact, the activities that the organization is able to put in place, are in most cases strictly related to the use of intangibles. Similarly, investing in the growth of IC would increase the sustainability of the organization: for example, investment in training and education for human resources is both relevant for the sustainability and the growth of IC. Effective management of human resources aimed at valuing employees' unique capabilities, is at the same time a practice of social responsibility and an action that increases the efficiency of human capital. A further advantage which will impact directly on value creation is to avoid intangible liabilities deriving from the loss of knowledge and high turnover of talents within the company. Again the development of collaborative practice both inside the organization and outside, with suppliers and partners, aimed at strengthening trust, reduces the potential unbalanced use of power among organizations in the supply chain (Drake and Schlachter 2008).

Scholars have already paid attention to this relationship, and through the technique of *casual mapping* which is designed to assist the performance measurement system of CSR related intangibles, have highlighted a financial evaluation on the return of investment aimed at increasing the value of CRS related intangibles (Schiuma and Lerro 2008).

Evaluating the idea that socially responsible behavior of the organization contributes to its long term financial sustainability and development, it is also possible to unveil the link between IC management and social responsibility in the pursuit of public value.

The previous discussion has highlighted how social responsibility is linked to IC management, in particular in regard to strategies supporting the internal development of knowledge and the professional growth of human resources, as well as to their interaction and ability in promoting relationships with different stakeholders. It goes without saying that this aspect is particularly relevant in public organizations, where people should be seen as co-producers in the public service delivery process (Osborne et al. 2013). Notwithstanding, the above condition and the progressive pervasive role of intangibles in the process of value creation and the recognition and management of these elements, still need to be integrated within the organization. This would be possible only through a process of organizational change, from which the use of a different tool to measure and recognize the interaction of all different elements concurring to the value creation process can result.

An issue to be discussed is how to disclose socially responsible behavior while disclosing action undertaken for the growth of IC. Although separate reports devoted to the disclosure of CSR as well as IC will be discussed in the chapter three, hereafter a point to address is if simply adding more information in financial reporting can result in appropriate accountability. As already discussed, traditional reporting systems are not suitable to fully capture the value of all IC components, and generally reflect only those that correspond to recognition.

Generally speaking, both for IC and for CSR actions two main problems arise while addressing disclosure:

- difficulties in quantifying their value (basically because of difficulties in isolating their value from others inside the organization);
- the need to contextualize them in the specific realm of the organization, looking at the strategic plan and the context in which it operates.

Scholars have proposed, in accordance with different theories (a clear synthesis in An et al. 2011) the positive role of voluntary disclosure, as a tool to improve the corporate image, attract capital (or reduce the cost of capitals) create a better understanding of products and services and from the utmost importance, improve the relationship with various stakeholders.

This kind of systematized disclosure could converge in one report, the IR, which can also address—especially for public organizations—the communication of other information relating to the mission and value creation process. In fact, it is worth noting that, apart from IC and sustainability reports, public organizations have also experienced a variety of reports which are different from those that have been discussed up until now, and are born in the public domain, having been intended to innovate budgeting and reporting in accordance to the logic of gender and participation (Bartocci and Picciaia 2013; Cohen and Karatzimas 2015). Gender reports are aimed at assessing and communicating action undertaken within the organization to offer equal opportunities to different social groups. They offer a reclassification of activities, revenues and expenditure occurred in one year focusing on social groups that can be consider relevant (e.g. female, elderly, young people, immigrants) (Grosser and Moon 2005). Participatory budgets can be considered as the tool institutionally prone to favour participatory democracy. It serves government in allowing people to participate in the budgeting process, thus empowering them in budgetary decisions (Zhang and Yang 2009). The inclusion of people in the decision making process is one of the constituent of Public Governance (Bovaird and Löffler 2009) and can be extended to public service delivery.

To conclude this section it is important to clarify that IR is not necessarily the evolution of a sustainability report and new adopters can also start their journey toward the preparation of IR by integrating different parts of the internal information system, including the internal control systems, and other forms of communication with different categories of stakeholders having been already adopted.

1.4 The Path: (Management) Accounting Process of Change

The overview undertaken on different accounting tools that has been widespread over the last decades makes it apparent that there is a need for more concise and clear forms of communication in addressing the different categories of stakeholders. However, especially in public organizations, stakeholders have a requirement to be involved actively in strategic decision making through a proper process of engagement: new forms of dialogue represent a prerequisite for a depth of stakeholder engagement. Based on these first considerations, the adoption of IR may represent the final solution as it juxtaposes different rationalities that nowadays represents the basis of new social order and "epitomises a practice in which different world views collide" (Van Bommel 2014).

Scholars have already discussed varieties of non-financial reporting in the aim of explaining the achievement of a legitimate agreement on their structure and adoption through the institutional lens (e.g. Bebbington et al. 2008; Brown et al. 2009; Larrinaga-Gonzalez 2007). However quite often the approach followed has been to examine the influence of different isomorphic pressures rather than a purposeful strategic process.

Organizations have been defined as social structures that are created by individuals aiming to support collaborative pursuits of specified goals (Scott 2003: 11). They are open systems that respond to change in the environment (Lawrence and Lorsch 1986). However, organizations operating in the same environment may receive different influences or may react in different ways to similar stimulus. It has also to be noted that changes do not occur from scratch, but progressively, and are strictly dependent on linkages between organizational settings and the wider environments carrying the institutions (Meyer 2008).

With these premises in mind, the lens that will be adopted in the examination of IR is still rooted in the institutional domain but will try to grasp how, inside the organization, changes occur in a way that creates the groundwork for integrated thinking, without which a sound IR would not exist.

As underlined by Perego et al., there is the need to understand IR as a "process of organizational learning both at field and organizational level" (2016: 28).

Referring to accounting systems it has been clarified by Miller and Power (2013) how accounting—even if profoundly technical in nature—is also, and at the same time, profoundly institutional, which is to say that styles and cultures may be quite stable and embedded in routines and work practices that can reinforce those styles.

Therefore, institutionalized change in a management accounting system requires a profound transformation in the existing routine as well as in the management accounting culture, allowing new forms of behaviour to evolve (Burns and Scapens 2000; Padovani et al. 2014). On the one hand, the decision to introduce a new accounting tool can create the right kind of pressure inside the organization's accounting practice, and as matter of fact, results from several components, such as ideas and routines, which in turn involve different actors into translating these ideas into performances (Miller and Power 2013). This is what Miller defines as the *mediating* role of accounting: "Accounting is also a mediating practice, meaning that it links up different actors with a common narrative and may constitute a network of relations within and beyond the boundaries of the enterprise" (Miller and Power 2013: 581).

The idea to examine the internal mechanisms and processes employed by the early adopter of IR has been already discussed by Stubbs and Higgins (2014) whom—based in the Laughlin's (1991) model of organisational change—aims to explore whether IR is stimulating innovative disclosure mechanisms.

In the present study the aim is slightly different: first of all the research is intended to study the on-going process of adoption of IR, thus investigating the step already taken in the case study analyzed, and also to foresee, together with relevant actors interviewed inside the organization, further steps to be completed. Some other studies have previously examined the mechanism employed in sustainability reporting (e.g. Adams and Frost 2008) finding out how the intention to adopt a different accountability tool has acted as a catalyst for organizational change through integrated sustainability performance data in strategic planning, decision making, risk management and performance measurement systems.

The case study chosen, triangulating documents, information available on the web and results of interviews, seek to verify to what extent, as already highlighted throughout the present chapter, the adoption of an integrated thinking required to progressively introduce a different approach to set strategies, objectives and measurement control tools, bearing in mind the full adoption of an integrated thinking before producing the IR.

1.5 The Tool: Integrated Reporting

The narrative of the present chapter allows us to consider the IR as the new frontier of communication both for private and public entities, but above all has emphasised that the IR should be the final step of a profound process of management change, thus avoiding to produce a document not coherent with strategies and the organization's culture.

The IR represents, from this point of view the results of a long and deep process of change that moves from a profound consideration of environmental policies implemented in the organization, the clear identification and consequent management of IC integrated with the consideration of traditional financial aspects.

While the consciousness of social and environmental responsibility to the protection of future generation has led to the development of the sustainability report (Bartocci and Picciaia 2013: 196), the need to make clear to all stakeholders the value creation process—also for a higher involvement of people as co-producers—brings us to create an innovative tool, the IR. The main aim is to discuss under an integrated approach, financial, social, environmental activities whilst discussing IC and human resources within the organization. The central focus of the IR is on the creation of value, which in a public organization should be declined as the creation of "*public value*", coherent with the inherent mission of any public organization. The concept of public value has been widely discussed by scholars, also through different perspectives and approaches (Benington 2009; Meynhardt 2009; Moore 1995; Talbot 2011). The definition given by Meynhardt (2009: 206) is: "Public value is what impacts on values about the 'public'". However, as it can appear tautological, in the aim of operationalizing the concept, in this work the point of reference is the encompassing definition offered by Benington (2009: 237), according to whom public value is:

- "*ecological value*—adding value to the public realm by actively promoting sustainable development and reducing public "bads" like pollution, waste, global warming;
- *political value*—adding value to the public realm by stimulating and supporting democratic dialogue and active public participation and citizen engagement;
- *economic value*—adding value to the public realm through the generation of economic activity and employment;
- *social and cultural value*—adding value to the public realm by contributing to social capital, social cohesion, social relationships, social meaning and cultural identity, individual and community well-being".

Of course "how" each kind of public organization can contribute to the creation of public value is a question that should be investigated in the specific context and articulated in accordance with the business model. However, the public value creation framework provided by Talbot (2011) which offers a scorecard to focus on five different aspects: *resources*, *services*, *social results*, *processes*, *trust and legitimacy*, can support the identification of strategies and objectives coherently with the concept of public value. What emerges from this discussion is that public value is the final result of several interconnected factors in which social environment, strategic choices and structures all play a role (Bartocci and Picciaia 2013) thus, IR represents a suitable tool to allow these interconnections to emerge. In particular the IR represents a suitable tool for state-owned enterprises, as several experience are already undergoing. But also non-market oriented public organization can benefit by the adoption of IR.

A point that characterizes IR and already embedded in sustainability reporting is the strong relationship with stakeholder engagement. This concept has been defined by Thomson and Bebbington as "a range of practices where organizations take a structured approach to consulting with potential stakeholders" (2005: 517). The idea is to create a dialogue with stakeholders to ascertain their view and expectation toward the entity (Rinaldi 2013). This approach is particularly eligible for public sector organizations, which have to gain legitimacy by their stakeholders and trust, through transparency and accountability. It would allow people to be co-producers of public services, involving them in decision-making (Bovaird 2007; Wiewiora et al. 2015) thus ensuring their needs are more accurately identified.

Furthermore, to discuss the suitability of adopting IR in public organization, it is worth considering the study by Eccles and Krzus (2010) whom for the first time have theorized the construction of "One Report" comprising of all relevant information under an integrated approach. As the authors highlight, the preparation of Integrated Reporting is rooted in practice, and scholars have provided a systematization to what has emerged. A large source of inspiration cited by Eccles and Krzus was the Annual report 2008 prepared by Philips, even if other companies before experimented this type of approach.[1]

Considering list of advantages that Eccles and Krzus (2010) identify in relation to the preparation of IR, there is a *greater clarity about relation and commitment*. This aspect is extremely relevant for any organization, but above all for public organizations which have at the core of their mission the production of public value, as previously specified. Thus, the general concept of value creation, which in public organizations should be "public value creation", needs to be articulated in clear objectives and related metrics, identifying the relationship between these key financial and non-financial metrics. Moreover, the possibility to compile all the different information and above all, to have an integrated approach while developing strategies related to sustainability, growth of intellectual capital, management of financial and tangible resources would also improve in relation to the different categories of stakeholders.

A further advantage should be a *better decision*: as underlined in management accounting literature, better measurement leads to better decisions (Atkinson et al. 1997; Epstein and Buhovac 2014). Thus, developing a set of metrics to clarify the coherence of strategies, objectives and action to the mission and vision of the organization should improve the ability to have a holistic approach in decision-making.

Deeper Engagement with all Stakeholders. As already noted engagement of both internal and external stakeholders is pivotal in preparing the IR and tends to create a convergence interest by stakeholders, whilst sending to all of them the same message. Of course engagement is not easy in public organizations that are dealing with a large plethora of stakeholders, but dialogue is at the core of the process. As highlighted by the KPMG report prepared for public sector (2012), stakeholder engagement can help the organization show how they have balanced the often conflicting needs of different stakeholder groups.

Lower Reputational Risk is a further advantage underlined by the authors, which has been echoed by a recent research undertaken by Ernest & Young (EY 2015) to investigate "what" investors are looking for. Outside the entity a better disclosure will enhance trust, while inside the entity the integrate thinking will reduce the risk of weak coordination.

All in all, Eccles and Krzus do not provide a specific model, even if they constantly underline the need to integrate sustainability reporting and disclosure, as

[1]In the chapter three the process that bring to the birth of a specific international framework addressing this new tool will be discussed.

well as all non-financial information (they include in this broad concept also intangibles) with the traditional financial reporting. To have a clear model we have to wait for the International Integrated Reporting Council (IIRC) that in 2013 proposed in the Consultation Draft of the Framework for Integrated Reporting, an encompassing tool to identify all elements that can eventually be included in integrated reporting.

The principle, concept and the model proposed by the IIRC will be discussed in the third chapter, after having outlined the process leading to the adoption of the framework. Of course the model would require a process of adjustment, considering the specific types of resources (so-called "capital" in the IIRC model) that each organization solidly use. Financial resource in a local government, for example, should be examined in relation to tax-decisions; at the same time proper information of spending decisions should be provided in a concise and understandable manner. While preparing the IR, in fact, it is important to bear in mind that people are the most significant users of information released by public organization: while politicians, investors, creditors, oversight and governing body looking at the information disclosed have the advantage of understanding financial figures, people need to have access to easily understandable financial information. In this regard, some scholars (Cohen and Karatzimas 2015) have already proposed to prepare a "popular integrated reporting". Despite the recommended "conciseness" of the IR, the document would possibly result in numerous pages, so the idea to prepare a report immediately suitable for everyone would improve accountability.

Authors discussing the future of IR have also considered two further relevant issues, that will be not examined in detail in this work but represent two further points to be addressed in future research: the relationship between the information disclosed on internet and assurance.

The internet nowadays represents an increasingly significant channel of communication for any organization, allowing to "open the door" to all possible stakeholders. Being stakeholders' engagement at the core of publication of IR, the internet has the potential to support communication and increase active participation for different groups of stakeholders. In this sense, Eccles and Krzus (2015) have done an empirical analysis investigating all companies that have already prepared an IR, discovering some of them use Websites to complement the printed version of IR adding more details on specific issue or video, interactive games and charts (like Novo Nordisk, Philips SAP).

In regard to *assurance*, some companies have it, who are part of the early adopters. An example comes from the case of Eskom, an electricity supplier in South Africa that in order to give more strength and ensure the reliability of information provided has obtained an external independent assurance statement, reported as Appendix to its IR, together with a Stakeholders' engagement matrix showing how different stakeholders have been involved in the preparation of IR (Granà and Ceccacci 2013).

A further point to discuss is *how* to move toward an integrated thinking in a public organization and, in the end, to the publication of an IR. In fact, the ultimate question is how to operationalize the "integrated thinking".

Interestingly, the Accountability for Sustainability (A4S) propose ten steps to move towards integrated thinking, generally addressing any kind of organization interested in adopting an integrated thinking in the adoption of sustainability strategies. In the public sector realm these steps can be similarly declined in order to ensure the linkages between the organization's strategy, governance and financial performance together with the social, environmental and economic context in which it operates.

1. *Board/councils and management commitment.* Subjects responsible for the governance of the organization should be conscious of the urgency of translating sustainability principles related to environment, growth of human resources and IC in a set of strategies coherent with financial and material resources available, in respect of a community's needs and searching for a sustainable development of community and environment;
2. *Understanding and analysing the key drive for public value creation* Public organizations manage public resources in the pursuit of creating public value. Considering framework related to sustainability issues and intellectual capital growth which can support and speed the process;
3. *Integrating the key public value creation drivers into the organization's strategy.* Having identified the key driver for public value creation and quantified their impact, they should be incorporated in the organization's strategy as an integrated part of the whole and not as stand-alone issues and objective;
4. *Ensuring that the approach to the public value creation is pervasive in the whole organization* (and not only in some departments). To fulfil the final mission a pivotal point is the clear consciousness by all employees and managers in the whole organization of objectives defined and related key drivers;
5. *Breaking down targets and objectives for the organization as a whole into targets and objectives which are meaningful for individual/divisions/departments.* Strategies should be translated into actions avoiding any gap between strategies and operating objectives;
6. *Processes that enable issues related to the public value creation to be taken into account clearly and consistently in day-to-day decision-making.* It is important to avoid any impediment that can be an obstacle to the realization of chosen strategies. Hence, Managers should have all authority, power and information to act in the pursuit of the chosen objectives.
7. *Extensive and effective sustainability training.* Promote a culture of sustainability, trust in the growth of human resources and IC in the pursuit of public value creation is fundamental for the success of integrated thinking. Training is key to this aspect and cynicism should be taken into account to raise awareness by any person engaged in the organization about the public value creation process.
8. *Including public value creation targets and objectives in performance appraisal.* All techniques useful to influence behaviour, including training, awareness raising, objective setting, remuneration, promotion and other incentives, should be adopted.

9. *Champions to promote public value creation and celebrate success.* People working at any level understanding strategies and objectives, deliberately need to be identified and an active involvement in integrating different issues relating to the public value creation has to be supported. Celebrating success can encourage further innovation within the organization.
10. *Monitoring and reporting performance in an integrated way.* Reporting results of strategies adopted in an integrated approach is essential to clarify both to internal and external stakeholders how the integrated thinking has operated.

To conclude the chapter a last question should be discussed: is IR the report of the future?

While discussing the future of reporting, participants in a research undertaken by the GRI have used the expression "Totally Integrated Report" referring to the report of the future (GRI 2015). Moreover, a Public Sector Pioneer Network has been created inside the IIRC to promote a conscious adoption of IR, exploring the connectivity of information that they are already publishing, and adopting an integrated thinking to improve the performance of public organizations.

However, scholars must play a relevant role in the next decade, supporting the development of integrated thinking as a prerequisite for the preparation of sound IR. Thus, profound processes of management change should occur before releasing the report: as data published revels (see IR examples database), companies publish an integrated report after years of sustainability reporting, thus empirically proving that the road towards the IR is long and winding one.

References

Abeysekera I (2013) A template for integrated reporting. J Intellect Capital 14(2):227–245

ACCA (Association of Chartered Certified Accountants) (2010) Sustainability reporting matters: what are national governments doing about it? London. UK. Available at http://www.accaglobal.com/content/dam/acca/global/PDF-technical/sustainability-reporting/tech-tp-srm.pdf. Accessed 9 June 2016

Adams C (2015) Understanding integrated reporting: The concise guide to integrated thinking and the future of corporate reporting. Do Sustainability, Oxford, UK

Adams CA, Frost GR (2008) Integrating sustainability reporting into management practices. Acc Forum 32(4):288–302

An Y, Davey H, Eggleton IR (2011) Towards a comprehensive theoretical framework for voluntary IC disclosure. J Intellect Capital 12(4):571–585

Andriessen D (2004) Making sense of intellectual capital: designing a method for the valuation of intangibles. Elsevier, Oxford UK

Arnaboldi M, Lapsley I (2009) On the implementation of accrual accounting: a study of conflict and ambiguity. European Acc Rev 18(4):809–836

Atkinson AA, Waterhouse JH, Wells RB (1997) A stakeholder approach to strategic performance measurement. MIT Sloan Manag Rev 38(3):25–37

Aucoin P (1990) Administrative reform in public management: paradigms, principles, paradoxes and pendulums. Governance 3(2):115–137

Ball A, Grubnic S, Birchall J (2014) Sustainability accounting and accountability in the public sector. In: Bebbington J, Unerman J, O'Dwyer B (eds) Sustainability accounting and accountability. Routledge, New York, pp 176–196

Bartocci L, Picciaia F (2013) The case of the auditor-general of South Africa. In: Busco C, Frigo ML, Riccaboni A, Quattrone P (eds) Integrated reporting: concepts and cases that redefine corporate accountability. Springer Science & Business Media. Springer International Publishing, Switzerland, pp 191–204

Benington J (2009) Creating the public in order to create public value? Int J Public Adm 32(3–4):232–249

Bebbington J, Larrinaga-González C, Moneva-Abadía JM (2008) Legitimating reputation/the reputation of legitimacy theory. Acc Auditing Accountability J 21(3):371–374

Birney A, Clarkson H, Madden P, Porritt J, Tuxworth B (2010) Stepping up: a framework for public sector leadership on sustainability. forum for the future. UK, London

Bontis N (1998) Intellectual capital: an exploratory study that develops measures and models. Manag Decis 36(2):63–76

Bontis N (2001) Assessing knowledge assets: a review of the models used to measure intellectual capital. Int J Manag Rev 3(1):41–60

Bovaird T (2005) Public governance: balancing stakeholder power in a network society. Int Rev Admin Sci 71(2):217–228

Bovaird T (2007) Beyond engagement and participation: user and community coproduction of public services. Public Adm Rev 67(5):846–860

Bovaird T, Löffler E (2009) Public management and governance. Routledge, New York, NY

Broadbent J, Guthrie J (1992) Changes in the public sector: a review of recent "alternative" accounting research. Acc Auditing & Accountability J 5(2):3–31

Bronzetti G, Sicoli G (2011) The application of intellectual capital reports in local authorities: Analysis and empirical evidence. Int J Knowl-Based Dev 2(1):85–106

Brown HS, de Jong M, Lessidrenska T (2009) The rise of the Global Reporting Initiative (GRI) as a case of institutional entrepreneurship. Environ Politics 18(2):182–200

Burns J, Scapens RW (2000) Conceptualizing management accounting change: an institutional framework. Manag Acc Res 11(1):3–25

Busco C, Frigo ML, Riccaboni A, Quattrone P (2013) Towards integrated reporting: concepts, elements and principles. In: Busco C, Frigo ML, Riccaboni A, Quattrone P (eds) Integrated reporting: concepts and cases that redefine corporate accountability. Springer Science & Business Media. Springer International Publishing, Switzerland, pp 3–18

Cañibano L, Garcia-Ayuso M, Sanchez P (2000) Accounting for intangibles: a literature review. J Acc Lit 19:102–130

Chen MC, Cheng SJ, Hwang Y (2005) An empirical investigation of the relationship between intellectual capital and firms' market value and financial performance. J Intellect Capital 6 (2):159–176

CIPFA (Chartered Institute of Public Finance and Accountancy) and Forum for the Future (2006) Sustainability: a reporting framework for the public services. CIPFA London, UK

Cohen S, Vlismas O (2013) Analyzing the relationship between intellectual capital and performance in local governments. Glob Bus Econ Rev 15:1–17

Cohen S, Karatzimas S (2015) Tracing the future of reporting in the public sector: introducing integrated popular reporting. Int J Public Sector Manag 28(6):449–460

Deegan C, Rankin M, Tobin J (2002) An examination of the corporate social and environmental disclosures of BHP from 1983-1997: a test of legitimacy theory. Acc Auditing Accountability J 15(3):312–343

Del Bello A (2006) Intangibles and sustainability in local government reports: An analysis into an uneasy relationship. J Intellect Capital 7(4):440–456

Drake MJ, Schlachter JT (2008) a virtue-ethics analysis of supply chain collaboration. J Bus Ethics 82(4):851–864

Drucker PF (1994) The theory of the business. Harvard Bus Rev 72(5):95–104

Druckman P, Fries J (2010) Integrated reporting: the future of corporate reporting? In: Eccles RG, Cheng B, Saaltzman D (eds) The landscape of integrated reporting. The President & Fellows of Harvard College, Massachusetts, pp 81–85

Dumay J, Guthrie J, Farneti F (2010) GRI sustainability reporting guidelines for public and third sector organizations: a critical review. Public Manag Rev 12(4):531–548

Dumay J, Guthrie J, Puntillo P (2015) IC and public sector: a structured literature review. J Intellect Capital 16(2):267–284

Eccles RG, Krzus MP (2010) One report. Integrated reporting for a sustainable society. Wiley, USA

Eccles RG, Krzus MP (with Sidney Ribot) (2015) The integrated reporting movement: meaning, momentum, motives, and materiality. Wiley, New Jersey

Eccles RG, Serafeim G (2014) Corporate and integrated reporting: a functional perspective. Working paper 14-094. Harvard Business School

Edvinsson L (2002) Corporate longitude. Bookhouse, Stockholm

Edvinsson L, Malone M (1997) Intellectual capital. Harper Business, New York

Epstein MJ, Buhovac AR (2014) Making sustainability work: Best practices in managing and measuring corporate social, environmental, and economic impacts. Berrett-Koehler Publishers, San Francisco

EY—Ernest & Young (2015) Tomorrow's investment rules 2.0 Emerging risk and stranded assets have investors looking for more from nonfinancial reporting. http://www.ey.com/Publication/vwLUAssets/EY-tomorrows-investment-rules-2/$FILE/EY-tomorrows-investment-rules-2.0.pdf. Accessed 8 May 2016

Fasan M (2013) Annual reports, sustainability reports and integrated reports: trends in corporate disclosure. In: Busco C, Frigo ML, Riccaboni A, Quattrone P (eds) Integrated reporting: concepts and cases that redefine corporate accountability. Springer Science & Business Media. Springer International Publishing, Switzerland, pp 41–57

Ferenhof HA, Durst S, Zaniboni Bialecki M, Selig PM (2015) Intellectual capital dimensions: state of the art in 2014. J Intellect Capital 16(1):58–100

Friedman M (1970) The social responsibility of business is to increase its profits. The New York Times Magazine, 13 Sept 1970

Granà F, Ceccacci F (2013) The case of eskom. In: Busco C, Frigo ML, Riccaboni A, Quattrone P (eds) Integrated reporting: concepts and cases that redefine corporate accountability. Springer Science & Business Media. Springer International Publishing, Switzerland, pp 297–311

Gray R (2006) Social, environmental and sustainability reporting and organisational value creation? Whose value? Whose creation? Acc Auditing Acc J 19(6):793–819

GRI (Global Reporting Initiative) (2005) Sector Supplement for Public Agencies, Amsterdam

GRI (Global Reporting Initiative) (2015) Sustainability and reporting Trends in 2025—Preparing the future. GRI's Reporting 2025 Project: First analysis paper, May 2015. Available at https://www.globalreporting.org/resourcelibrary/Sustainability-and-Reporting-Trends-in-2025-1.pdf. Accessed 10 June 2016

Grimmelikhuijsen S, Porumbescu G, Hong B, Im T (2013) The effect of transparency on trust in government: a cross-national comparative experiment. Public Adm Rev 73(4):575–586

Grosser K, Moon J (2005) Gender mainstreaming and corporate social responsibility: reporting workplace issues. J Bus Ethics 62(4):327–340

Grüber S (2014) Intangible values in financial accounting and reporting: an analysis from the perspective of financial analysts. Fachmedien Wiesbaden, Switzerland, Springer

Guthrie J (2001) The management, measurement and the reporting of intellectual capital. J Intellect Capital 2(1):27–41

Guthrie J, Dumay J (2015) New frontiers in the use of intellectual capital in the public sector. J Intellect Capital 16(2):258–266

Guthrie J, Farneti F (2008) GRI sustainability reporting by Australian public sector organizations. Public Money Manag 28(6):361–366

Guthrie J, Olson O, Humphrey C (1999) Debating developments in new public financial management: the limits of global theorising and some new ways forward. Fin Accountability Manag 15(3–4):209–228

Guthrie J, Humphrey C, Jones LR, Olson O (2005) International public financial management reform: progress, contradictions, and challenges. IAP. Greenwich, Connetticut

Higgins C, Stubbs W, Love T (2014) Walking the talk(s): organisational narratives of integrated reporting. Acc Auditing Accountability J 27(7):1090–1119

Hood C (1991) A public management for all seasons? Public Adm 69(1):3–19

Hood C (1995) The "New Public Management" in the 1980s: variations on a theme. Acc Organ Soc 20(2):93–109

Hoque Z, Moll J (2001) Public sector reform—Implications for accounting, accountability and performance of state-owned entities-an Australian perspective. Int J Public Sector Manag 14 (4):304–326

IIRC (2013) Consultation draft of the international <IR> framework. IIRC, London

Jensen JC, Berg N (2012) Determinants of traditional sustainability reporting versus integrated reporting. An institutionalist approach. Bus Strategy Environ 21(5):299–316

KPMG (2012) Applying integrated reporting principles in the public sector. Available at https://home.kpmg.com/content/dam/kpmg/pdf/2013/04/applying-ir-principles.pdf. Accessed 11 June 2016

Larrinaga-Gonzalez C (2007) Sustainability reporting: insights from neo-institutional theory. In: Unerman J, Bebbington J, O'Dwyer B (eds) Sustainability accounting and accountability. Routledge. London, pp 150–167

Laughlin RC (1991) Environmental disturbances and organizational transitions and transformations: some alternative models. Organ Stud 12(2):209–232

Lawrence PR, Lorsch JW (1986) Organization and environment: managing differentiation and integration. Harvard Business School Classics

Lev B (2001) Intangibles: management, measurement, and reporting. Brookings Institute Press, Washington DC

Lev B, Cañibano L, Marr B (2005) An accounting perspective on intellectual capital. In: Marr B (ed) Perspectives on Intellectual Capital, Oxford, pp 42–55

Lewis L (2000) Environmental audits in local government: a useful means to progress in sustainable development. Acc Forum 24(3):296–318

Mack J, Ryan C (2007) Is there an audience for public sector annual reports: Australian evidence? Int J Public Sector Manag 20(2):134–146

Maditinos D, Chatzoudes D, Tsairidis C, Theriou G (2011) The impact of intellectual capital on firms' market value and financial performance. J Int Capital 12(1):132–151

Manes-Rossi F, Citro F, Bisogno M (2016) Intellectual capital in action: evidence from italian local governments. J Int Capital 17(4) forthcoming

Massingham PR, Tam L (2015) The relationship between human capital, value creation and employee reward. J Int Capital 16(2):390–418

Matten D, Moon J (2008) "Implicit" and "explicit" CSR: a conceptual framework for a comparative understanding of corporate social responsibility. Acad Manag Rev 33(2):404–424

Meritum (2002) Guidelines for managing and reporting on intangibles (intellectual capital report). Vodafore Foundation. Available at http://www.pnbukh.com/files/pdf_filer/MERITUM_Guidelines.pdf. Accessed 12 June 2016

Meyer JW (2008) Reflections on institutional theories of organizations. In: Greenwood R, Oliver C, Suddaby R, Sahlin-Andersson K (eds) The Sage handbook of organizational institutionalism. Sage, London, pp 790–811

Meynhardt T (2009) Public value inside: What is public value creation? Int J Public Adm 32 (3–4):192–219

Miller P, Power M (2013) Accounting, organizing, and economizing: connecting accounting research and organization theory. Acad Manag Ann 7(1):557–605

Moore MH (1995) Creating public value: strategic management in government. Harvard University Press, USA

Mouritsen J, Larsen HT, Bukh PND (2001) Intellectual capital and the 'capable firm': narrating, visualising and numbering for managing knowledge. Acc Organ Soc 26(7):735–762
Mussari R, Monfardini P (2010) Practices of social reporting in public sector and non-profit organizations: An Italian perspective. Public Manag Rev 12(4):487–492
Nahapiet J, Ghoshal S (1998) Social capital, intellectual capital, and the organizational advantage. Acad Manag Rev 23(2):242–266
Olson O, Guthrie J, Humphrey C (eds) (1998) Global warning, debating international developments in new public financial management. Cappelen Akademisk, Oslo
Osborne SP, Radnor Z, Nasi G (2013) A new theory for public service management? Toward a (public) service-dominant approach. Am Rev Public Adm 43(2):135–158
Osborne SP, Radnor Z, Vidal I, Kinder T (2014) A sustainable business model for public service organizations? Public Manag Rev 16(2):165–172
Padovani E, Orelli RL, Young DW (2014) Implementing change in a hospital management accounting system. Public Manag Rev 16(8):1184–1204
Perego P, Kennedy S, Whiteman G (2016) A lot of icing but little cake? Taking integrated reporting forward. J Cleaner Prod forthcoming. 10.1016/j.jclepro.2016.01.106
Petty R, Guthrie J (2000) Intellectual capital literature review: measurement, reporting and management. J Intellect Capital 1(2):155–176
Pollitt C, Bouckaert G (2011) Public management reform: a comparative analysis-new public management, governance, and the Neo-Weberian State. Oxford University Press, New York
Ramírez Y (2010) Intellectual capital models in Spanish public sector. J Intellect Capital 11 (2):248–264
Rinaldi L (2013) Stakeholder engagement. In: Busco C, Frigo ML, Riccaboni A, Quattrone P (eds) Integrated reporting: concepts and cases that redefine corporate accountability. Springer Science & Business Media. Springer International Publishing, Switzerland, pp 95–109
Robb SWG, Single LE, Zarzeski MT (2001) Non-financial disclosure across Anglo-American countries. J Int Acc Auditing Taxation 10(1):71–83
Robertson FA, Samy M (2015) Factors affecting the diffusion of integrated reporting—a UK FTSE 100 perspective. Sustain Acc Manag Policy J 6(2):190–223
Rowbottom N, Locke J (2016) The emergence of <IR>. Acc Bus Res 46(1):83–115
Schiuma G, Lerro A (2008) Intellectual capital and company's performance improvement. Measuring Bus Excellence 12(2):3–9
Scott WR (2003) Organizations. Relational, natural, and open systems. Pearson. Upper Saddle River. New Jersey
Secundo G, Elena-Perez S, Martinaitis Z, Leitner KH (2015) An intellectual capital maturity model (ICMM) to improve strategic management in European universities: A dynamic approach. J Intellect Capital 16(2):419–442
Serrano Cinca C, Molinero CM, Queiroz AB (2003) The measurement of intangible assets in public sector using scaling techniques. J Intellect Capital 4(2):249–275
Steurer R (2010) The role of governments in corporate social responsibility: Characterising public policies on CSR in Europe. Policy Sci 43(1):49–72
Stubbs W, Higgins C (2014) Integrated reporting and internal mechanisms of change. Acc Auditing Accountability J 27(7):1068–1089
Talbot C (2011) Paradoxes and prospects of 'public value'. Public Money Manag 31(1):27–34
Thomas JC (2012) Citizen, customer, partner: engaging the public in public management, M. E. Sharpe. New York
Thomson I, Bebbington J (2005) Social and environmental reporting in the UK: a pedagogic evaluation. Crit Perspect Acc 16(5):507–533
Van Bommel K (2014) Towards a legitimate compromise? An exploration of integrated reporting in the Netherlands. Acc Auditing Accountability J 27(7):1157–1189
Walker RG (2009) Public sector consolidated statements—An assessment. Abacus 45(2):171–220
Wayne SU (2001) Business and financial reporting: challenges from the new economy. Financial Accounting Series. 219/A

Wiewiora A, Keast R, Brown K (2015) Opportunities and challenges in engaging citizens in the co-production of infrastructure-based public services in Australia. Public Manag Rev 18(4):1–25

World Bank (2008) Environmental sustainability an evaluation of world bank group support. Washington. http://siteresources.worldbank.org/EXTENVIRONMENT/Resources/environ_eval.pdf. Accessed 4 June 2016

Zambon S (2004) Intangibles and intellectual capital: an overview of the reporting issues and some measurement models. In: Bianchi P, Labory S (eds) The economic importance of intangible assets. Ashgate. Aldershot, pp 153–83

Zhang Y, Yang K (2009) Citizen participation in the budget process: the effect of city managers. J Budgeting, Acc Fin Manag 21(2):289–317

Chapter 2
Accounting Change: Integrated Reporting Through the Lenses of Institutional Theory

Abstract Institutional theory has been largely adopted in accounting studies to frame research. The chapter explores Management Accounting Change as a lens to observe how the isomorphic and intra organizational dynamics interact, driving towards the adoption of the Integrated Reporting. More specifically, drawing on various Institutional theory strands such as New Institutional theory and Old Institutional Economics, complementary with change management theories, a complete theoretical framework is formulated. This approach intends to grasp—through a deep understanding of institutions, routines and change, both planned and unplanned and to what extent accounting change is related to the adoption of Integrated Reporting. For these reasons the case study presented in the last chapter is intended to analyse the process started in a public sector organization towards the adoption of the Integrated Reporting, by showing the undergoing management accounting change process.

Keywords Integrated reporting · Management accounting change · Institutional theory · Old institutional economics · New institutional sociology · Routines

2.1 Accounting Change: An Institutional Perspective

The present chapter explores the phenomenon of accounting change with respect to the use of Integrated Reporting (IR) in public sector entities, in an attempt to gain a better understanding of how the isomorphic and intra organizational dynamics interact and influence the process of accounting change on both the macro and micro levels. Scholars have widely discussed the fact that studying accounting change cannot be limited to the consideration of techniques and related effects, generated by the environment or by specific agents of change. On the contrary, it needs to take into account the processual dynamic of these changes and the related effects on organizations (Laughlin 1991; Broadbent and Guthrie 1992; Larrinaga

This chapter was written by Epameinondas Katsikas.

E. Katsikas et al., *Towards Integrated Reporting*,
SpringerBriefs in Accounting, DOI 10.1007/978-3-319-47235-5_2

and Bebbington 2001; Contrafatto and Burns 2013). The attempted change depends on the activation and interaction of the isomorphic forces as well as on the intra organizational dynamics that guided the overall change process, from the starting point to its end, resulting in the uprising of new daily accounting practices and routines.

The phenomenon of change and its complexity has guided the adoption of a theoretical triangulation. Several scholars call for the use of multiple theories to discuss the role of different actors, practices, routines as well as institutional factors in accounting change (Modell 2007; Hoque et al. 2013). In the current research, the adoption of a theoretical triangulation supports a thorough understanding and explanation of the phenomenon under investigation from different perspectives and levels, such as the institutional and managerial approaches on a macro and micro level. Drawing on various Institutional theory strands such as the New Institutional theory and Old Institutional Economics complementary with change management theories, a complete theoretical framework is formulated. It will facilitate the understanding of accounting change as it relates to the adoption of IR. In particular, New Institutional theory perspectives were employed in order to interpret the dynamics of accounting change on a macro level of analysis, whilst Old Institutional Economics and managerial approaches were combined to advance a complete explanation of the dynamics of accounting change at a micro organizational level.

According to Lapsley and Wright (2004), the adoption of accounting innovations from public organizations is highly influenced by governmental policy. Isomorphic forces such as coercive, normative and mimetic ones have been slightly activated by the external environment, in order to direct public entities towards the adoption of IR, while a stronger pressure has been exerted on the private domain.

Furthermore, public entities are complex social and activity systems. They are mainly characterised as bureaucratic organizations that operate within a dynamic environment: attempts to change these organizations through legislative reforms are not always effective in terms of change (Brunsson and Sahlin-Andersson 2000). Institutionalized change in a management accounting system requires a profound transformation in the existing routine as well as in management accounting culture, thus allowing new forms of behaviour to evolve (Burns and Scapens 2000; Padovani et al. 2014).

Bearing in mind these premises, this chapter reviews the literature on Institutional theory and its various strands, as well as the most relevant theories of management accounting change. Light is shed on issues such as the reasons behind accounting change, the driving and embeddedness of dynamics and their interactions, phase models of change toward gaining a successful insight into the comprehension of the processes driving the adoption of IR. The following section discusses institutional theory and the rationale behind the adoption of institutional theory assumptions. It discusses the different institutional approaches and strands from an alignment to this study perspective and the way they relate to the research area. The third section discusses management accounting change in terms of its nature and reviews the preconditions and processes of change. The last section focuses on the processes of change, and on gaining a better understanding of the different stages of change towards the successful organizational response and reaction for the introduction of IR. Finally, it discusses the common sense which derives from analysis identified above.

2.1.1 Institutional Theory

Institutional theory is not merely one theory, but a wide range of different views of organized human behaviour. These different views have in common the assumption that human action is in some way constrained by social structure, which is the product of past social interactions. Institutional theory challenges the idea of the economically rational actor, who can freely select the optimal action alternative, without considering the restrictions posed by the social environment of which the actor is a part. It regards the actor's action choices for a large part contingent on the norms, values and habits embedded in his social setting. Institutional theory attends to the deeper and more resilient aspects of social structure. It considers the processes by which structures, rules, norms, and routines, become established and institutionalized as authoritative guidelines for social behaviour. It also delves into how these elements are created, diffused, adopted, and adapted over space and time, and how they fall into decline and disuse.

2.1.2 Why Institutional Theory

Action and change in organisations and their environments are central to this study. Organizations, "are groups of individuals bound together by some common purpose to achieve certain objectives" (North 1990, p. 5). Organisations are viewed as open systems (Scott 1998) in contact with their environment. They are part of an organisational field in which they are subject to the influences of institutions (DiMaggio and Powell 1991a, b; Scott 2001b). Organizations can be treated as actors in some circumstances but generally can be regarded as institutions. Indeed, under some conditions, organizations can be treated as single economic actors, but the inevitable existence of rules within organizations means that organizations must be regarded as a type of institution (Hodgson 2007). During the last two decades, organizational researchers have paid significant attention to the study of organizational action from several perspectives including contingency theory (Mintzberg 1979, 1981; Miller and Friesen 1984), population ecology (Hannan and Freeman 1977, 1984), resource dependence (Pfeffer and Salancik 1978), and various strands of institutional theory such as transaction cost economics (Williamson 1985), New Institutional Sociology (Meyer and Rowan 1977; DiMaggio and Powell 1983; DiMaggio and Powell 1991a, b; Meyer and Rowan 1991; Mouritsen 1994) and Old Institutional Economics (Hodgson 1993). Furthermore, organizational change has been studied in several modes across a plethora of discipline areas, and has been theorized using a variety of lenses, including institutional theory (Brignall and Modell 2000; Burns and Scapens 2000; Ribeiro and Scapens 2006). Dacin et al. (2002) state that "institutional theory has risen to prominence as a popular and powerful explanation for both individual and organisational action" and it can help to indicate factors that influence how organisations respond to change. Institutional theory has evolved into a body of literature encompassing multiple levels of analysis concerning change throughout organisations. It deals with how organisations are affected by forces that lie beyond their control (Hoffman 1999) and is built on the notion that institutional environments are socially constructed (DiMaggio and Powell 1983). According to this view, the institutional environment and its participants play key roles in shaping organisational systems, structures and behaviours. Institutional theorists suggest that institutional theory can be applied to a variety of different organisations and many different levels of analysis, stretching from a macro-system perspective to an organisational sub-system perspective (Scott 2001a, b). Institutional theory has been adopted to explain changes in accounting practices and to clarify the influence of these practices on institutional and organizational change (Dillard et al. 2004).

Consistently, institutional theory has also proven its explanatory power in earlier research on IR showing that it can constitute a useful framework for studying the response to external pressure in the process of the adoption of IR (Jensen and Berg 2012; Frías-Aceituno et al. 2013; Wild and van Staden 2013). More specifically, Jensen and Berg (2012) adopted this lens to discuss determinants of IR, with a focus on the elements that can favour an integrated approach rather than maintaining separate reporting on corporate social and environmental accountability, raising questions about how corporate social responsibility is embedded in the strategic planning process of an entity and why organisations adopt IR. Frías-Aceituno et al. (2013) examine the institutional factors—and in particular the role played by the legal system—that drives some leading companies to adopt IR as a communication tool which expresses the interconnections between organizational strategy, governance, performance and prospects, as well as the contexts in which they operate (p. 45). Wild and van Staden (2013) recall New Institutional theory as a valuable lens to comprehend motivations and drivers of institutional change, with regard to the understanding of shifts in accounting behaviour. Thus, in the following paragraphs institutional theory and an explanation for accounting change under this perspective are discussed.

2.1.3 Institutions, Routines and Change

Institutional theorists study the role of institutions in society. Institutions are complex, functionally differentiated systems that consist of multiple elements and components. They are defined as: "a way of thought or action of some prevalence and permanence, which is embedded in the habits of a group or the customs of a people" (Burns and Scapens 2000, p. 5). According to North (1990, p. 3) "Institutions are the rules of the game in a society", or more formally, the humanly devised constraints that shape interaction and reduce uncertainty by providing a structure to everyday life. Boons and Strannegård (2000, p. 9) define institutions as "action patterns that have become taken for granted within an organizational field". Repeated actions are turning into institutions, which consequently influence organizations. Thus, Burns and Scapens (2000) consider institutions as underlying behaviour, while Boons and Strannegård (2000) depict institutions as the behaviour itself.

Furthermore, Djelic and Quack (2003) propose that institutions have both a structural dimension, including formal and informal rules and systems, and an agency dimension, including action patterns. The most visible formal rules are the laws enacted by a legitimate body representing the common interests of the people. The formal rules stand on a foundation of taken for granted rules which constitute the informal institutions of society. Also, North (1990) has proposed a distinction between formal and informal institutions. Formal institutions constitute rules and laws such as constitutions and regulatory systems, while the informal institutions constitute norms of behaviour, conventions, and self-imposed codes of conduct. Formal institutions are enforced by the state or by a superior authority, whereas informal institutions are more likely to be enforced by the members of a society. Formal and informal institutions also differ in the pace with which they change. The majority of literature treats informal institutions as a source of resistance, rather than a resource for change (North 1990; Eggertsson 1996; Shaw 1997; Williamson 2000). They are believed to possess a certain inertia that slows down the process of change and hence, are often taken for granted. North (1990) argued that although informal institutional change can be an extremely lengthy process, institutions could change via collapse, replacement by another informal institution, or replacement by a formal institution. In contrast, formal institutions have been pointed out as a locus of opportunity for change (Ostrom 1999; Williamson 2000). Formal institutions change easier and more effectively than informal ones. For instance, in his hierarchy of institutions, where the higher levels are less liable to change than the lower ones, Williamson (2000) places formal bodies at the second level, whereas informal institutions lie at the first level. Formal institutions may change in different ways, for instance they can change in terms of formal institutional design, or in terms of formal institutional strength (Williamson 2000).

The concept of institutions is often associated with that of organizational routines. Pentland et al. (2010, p. 917) discussed that research on organizational routines is "still struggling with how to conceptualize, observe and compare [...] organisational routines". Routines are considered as including everything that is stored, maintained and developed in the organization, and which is the ultimate key to its survival (Jones and Craven 2001). Hodgson (2008, p. 19) stated that "routines are not behaviour; they are stored capacities or capabilities". Literature of routinized behaviour investigates routines at a micro level perspective, emphasizing the cognitive process of individuals and at a macro level perspective emphasizing structural and institutional constraints. In contrast with the view that organizational routines are a source of inertia (Hannan and Freeman 1989) has considered them as a source of change as well as stability (Burns and Scapens 2000; Feldman and Pentland 2003; Quinn 2010). Feldman and Pentland (2003, p. 96) characterize them as "a repetitive, recognizable pattern of interdependent actions, involving multiple actors" that are an accretion of organizational practices.

Beyond any question, there is a strong connection between institutions and organizational routines. By being an essential part of organizations, routines constitute the inner content of an institution, since they execute the same role of compiling rules and norms. Boons and Strannegård (2000) have provided a definition which points out the role of routines in institutions. Institutions, they claim, "are to be understood as action patterns that have become taken for granted within an organizational field. Repeated actions turn into institutions that, in turn, exert influence on organizations" (p. 9). However, the role of routines for institutions has been quite varied. More recent studies claim that routines have the capacity to enable or inhibit organizational or institutional change (Feldman 2000; Howard-Grenville 2005). As routines are dynamic, people's reflections on and reactions to the outcomes of routines can change the routines, which eventually may lead to institutional transformation (Feldman 2000). Hodgson (2007) has labelled routines as the key mechanism for institutional transformation. Lounsbury and Crumley (2007) have investigated how innovation in activities may lead to the establishment of a new practice via institutionalization. They argue that a practice is best understood as a kind of institution and can provide insightful knowledge about the origins of institutional transformation. The mechanism of reciprocal action between routines and institutional innovation takes the form of translation of macro institutes to the micro level forms and reversely from the micro level to the macro one. A routine can both shape and be shaped by the institution that governs its organizational activity. Institutions themselves evolve through a process of routinization of human activity (Burns and Scapens 2000) and routines themselves can be institutionalized (Barley and Tolbert 1997). The institutionalization of a routine implies that over time it can come to support the "taken-for-granted" ways of thinking and doing of particular organizations (Mouritsen 1994).

"If the nature of actors and their modes of acting are constituted and constrained by institutions, how can these actors change the very institutions in which they are embedded?" (Scott 2001b). This question seems to indicate that institutional change may not be possible; along this line, earlier research using an institutional approach was focussed more on persistence rather than on change (Oliver 1992; Stensaker 2004). However, it is supported that "although institutions function to provide stability and order, they themselves undergo change, both incremental and revolutionary" (Scott 2001a). Some authors also speak of deinstitutionalisation, meaning that legitimacy of an established institution erodes or discontinues, after which a new institution can come into place, possibly replacing the old institution (Oliver 1992; Scott 2001b).

North (1990) described changes in institutions with the help of a sports metaphor. Rules can constrain players, but sometimes one can get away with breaking the rules. This depends on the monitoring of these rules. The purpose of the rules is to define the way the game is played. However, the rules of the game can be changed due to external factors, advertisers who want the game to be more attractive for example, but also due to internal factors such as teams because the new rules suit them better than the existing ones. Following this metaphor, institutional change can thus be caused by factors exogenous as well as endogenous to the institution. Possible external factors leading to changes in institutions are the introduction of new technologies, major changes in policies, major political upheavals, social reform, economic crises or dislocations and shifts in cultural beliefs and practices (Scott 2001b).

The state is perceived as one of the major sources of stability or change, as it can define the rules of the game (Fligstein 1991). Governments clearly play a strategic role in institutional change, having the capacity to influence both positively and negatively the restructuring of national institutions as facilitators or inhibitors of institutional change (Pearce 2001; Djelic and Quack 2003). Facilitating governments are supportive of organizations, and provide predictable laws and regulations that these governments are capable of enforcing. For example, under the EU pressure and transitional aspirations, governments were a significant force triggering the import of new institutions to transitional contexts (Djelic and Quack 2003). Governments that are less facilitative are less supportive of organizations, more erratic and weaker. An ineffective or non-facilitative government creates an environment characterized by greater uncertainty (Pearce 2001).

2.2 Institutional Approaches: An Overview

In the literature, institutional approaches have been divided into three categories, which are titled as New Institutional Economics (Foster and Ward 1994), New Institutional Sociology (Carruthers 1995; Covaleski et al. 1996) and Old Institutional Economics (Scapens 1994; Burns and Scapens 2000). The focus of this study is on the two latter perspectives as both facilitate and guide this research and contribute to the formulation of the theoretical framework. Before discussing the specifics of each strand, two common underpinning assumptions should be noted. Firstly, institutional theory is built on the belief that institutional environments are socially constructed; that is, they are a human fabrication (Meyer and Rowan 1977; DiMaggio and Powell 1983; DiMaggio and Powell 1991a). Secondly, institutional theory takes the view that organisations are open systems. This suggests that the external environment and its participants help to shape organisational structures and activities (Scott 1998). Scott (1998, p. 21) sums up this view by explaining that "Every organisation exists in a specific physical, technological, cultural and social environment to which it must adapt. No organisation is self-sufficient; all depend for survival on types of relations they establish with larger systems of which they are a part."

Thus, from an institutional perspective, organisations operate in an environment dominated by rules, taken-for-granted assumptions and routines about what constitutes appropriate or acceptable organisational forms and behaviour (Meyer and Rowan 1977; DiMaggio and Powell 1991a, b). This institutional environment is viewed as defining not only the appropriate organisational systems, structures and behaviours but also the manner in which they conform to institutionalised beliefs in society. In general, this perspective assumes that the institutional environment constrains the organisation and determines its internal structure and, consequently, the behaviour of the actors in the organisation (DiMaggio and Powell 1983).

The next section describes the Old Institutional Economics and then the New Institutional Sociology perspectives. The differences between the two strands are not so deep but are still relevant. While the latter is concerned with the institutions in the organisational environment that shape structures and systems, the former is concerned with the institutions that shape the actions and thoughts of individual human agents (Scapens 2006).

2.2.1 Old Institutional Economics: The Concept

Old Institutional Economics' theory challenged the concept of the "rational economic man" suggesting that economic activities are not necessarily outcomes of rational decision-making but are products of the social environment (Hodgson 1998; Parto 2005; Vatn 2005). Typically, Old Institutional Economics believes that individuals' behaviour and the mechanism of the market are both significantly influenced by the institutional context; and the latter, it argues, requires a theoretical explanation in its own right. Old Institutional Economics theory supposes that the individuals and organizations' actions are determined by the socially learned and acceptable behavioural patterns (Nelson 1994; Hodgson 1998; Abdul Khalid 2000). However, being influenced by the institutional context does not mean that individuals are passive. Rather, both individual behaviour and societal norms are mutually reinforcing; they both influence and are influenced by each other (Hodgson 1993; Dugger and Sherman 1994). In addition, individual behaviour is seen to be driven by habit. When habits become part of group actions, they can evolve into routines and customs (Hodgson 1998). Hodgson (1998) links the concept of habits with the notion of institutions. The theory suggests that institutions are ways to support the interests and handle the conflicts amongst various individuals, organisations or groups and the wider environmental forces and actors (Vatn 2005). Therefore, from the Old Institutional Economics viewpoint, institutions embrace settled ways of thinking and doing, which are common to a specific community/group (Burns and Scapens 2000). For Old Institutional Economics researchers, the adoption of new structures, systems and behaviour in organizations would be seen to be strongly influenced by politics, society, and the cultural environment. Such institutionalists contend that the adoption of change might be a potential source of conflict and resistance. The implementation of new systems will succeed to the extent that there is broad congruence between the new systems and existing routines and institutions in companies. That is, the adoption and successful implementation or rejection and resistance to change of a new system and practice is dependent on whether the norms and values underpinning their adoption and implementations are in accordance with the norms and values of actors in organizations, those who are going to adopt, implement and use it. Old Institutional Economics perspective is more about why and how particular systems and practices emerge, sustain and/or change over time i.e., the dynamics of the change process rather than the outcomes of a change event (Burns 2001). As Scapens (1994) argues, it is more fruitful to use the Old Institutional Economics framework to understand the processes of change, change facilitators and resistance to change. This framework highlights institutions (with habits, and routines as their building blocks) at individuals, groups, firms and/or society levels of analysis and focuses on both formal (rules based) and informal (tacit/cognitive-level) aspects of institutions (Burns 2001). Accordingly, and also in summary, an Old Institutional Economics approach would more directly consider why and how such organizations activities emerged and are sustained and/or changed over time.

However, an organization's survival requires it to conform to societal norms of acceptable practice in order to achieve high levels of production efficiency and effectiveness. From the New Institutional Sociology perspective, the success of an organization is defined to the extent to which the organization embodies societal ideals concerning norms of rational behaviour. From this point of view, more societal legitimacy can be achieved by more conformity to societal norms. This legitimacy, which affects the organization structure defining its domain of activity, is the main factor in the survival and growth of an organization (Meyer and Scoot 1992). This could be considered the reason for the adoption of IR, which in a few years has emerged and established worldwide (Rowbottom and Locke 2016).

2.2.2 *New Institutional Sociology*

During the last two decades in particular, researchers have increasingly adopted New Institutional Sociology to assist them in conceptualising and explaining organizational actions and practices. It is because of its challenge to conventional wisdom and the prevailing research beliefs that assert that organizations are bounded, relatively autonomous and made up of rational actors (Abernethy and Chua 1996; Baxter and Chua 2003). The foundations of New Institutional Sociology were laid by Meyer and Rowan's (1977), who had identified inconsistencies and observed the loose coupling of formal structures/procedures and actual work practices, which existing organisational theory could not explain (Meyer and Scott 1992). In comparison to the previous approaches on the study of organisations, New Institutional Sociology provides an enriched conceptualisation of the environment and how this may impinge on organisations. However, it still conceptualises organisations as actors that respond in a relatively unified fashion to environmental stimuli or to pressures from the networks in which they are involved (Ribeiro and Scapens 2006). New Institutional Sociology views organizations as embedded within larger inter organizational networks and cultural systems. This institutional environment not only influences the organization's input and output markets but also its beliefs, norms and historical traditions. Furthermore, the institutional environment is characterised by the elaboration of rules, practices, symbols, beliefs, and normative requirements to which individual organizations must conform to receive support and legitimacy (Abernethy and Chua 1996). The success of an organization from a New Institutional Sociology perspective is defined by the extent to which it embodies societal ideals regarding norms of rational behaviour. New Institutional Sociology maintains that an organization's internal and formal structures and processes, that is, all the procedures, rules and routines defining how the organization's activities need to be carried out in order to achieve its goals, are formed by its external wider social environment/societal, institutionalised rules (Scott and Meyer 1983; Meyer and Rowan 1991; Scott 1991) rather than overriding internal aims for cost-minimisation or internal technical requirements. New Institutional Sociology has been utilised by researchers in order to explain why some organisations that exist in highly institutional environments appear to be similar. According to this, organisations tend to follow the formal structures and procedures that are valued in their social and cultural environment in order to achieve legitimacy and to secure the resources that are essential for their survival (McKinley and Mone 2003; Ribeiro and Scapens 2006). This search for legitimacy and resources leads organisations to adopt the most visible formal structures and procedures that are diffused within their social and cultural environment. Organizations operating in similar environments are said to experience comparable demands over what is generally regarded as being acceptable behaviour and, consequently, will have similar structures and processes (DiMaggio and Powell 1991b). An organization that conforms to societal rules obtains external legitimacy and increases its chance for survival, irrespective of whether new rules or procedures would make the organization more effective (Carpenter and Feroz 2001). Thus, being efficient is not the only way that organizations can survive. Legitimacy in the external environment that is from the state, the government, the parent companies and other external bodies, is another means of ensuring survival (Carruthers 1995). Such congruence in organizational structures and processes, grounded by the pressures of environmental expectations and beliefs, is said to have emerged through a process of isomorphism (DiMaggio and Powell 1991b). Isomorphism is "a constraining process that forces one unit in a population to resemble other units that face the same set of environmental conditions" (DiMaggio and Powell 1983, p. 149). DiMaggio and Powell (1991a, b) identify three mechanisms through which institutional isomorphic change occurs and through which organizations adopt systems and procedures, each with its own antecedents: coercive, normative and mimetic. These reflect the three pillars of institutions (Scott 2001b) that we conceive of as a continuum ranging from rigid approaches to subtle interventions. The regulative, normative, and cultural-cognitive pillars are the three analytical elements that make up or support institutions. Each element operates through its own mechanisms and processes. Distinguishing between the different analytical elements or pillars should help identify the processes taking place and the different pressures that institutions can exert. However, as Scott (2001b) also acknowledges, in reality the distinction between the pillars is not always that strict; in reality, inter-pillar communication is possible. Rules and regulations are almost by definition part of institutional theory; institutions are seen to provide structure just as rules and regulations. According to Scott (2001b), the regulatory process in the sense of the regulative pillar concerns "the capacity to establish rules, inspect others' conformity to them, and, as necessary, manipulate sanctions—rewards or punishments—in an attempt to influence future behaviour" (p. 52).

The regulative institutional pillar represents the rules and the laws of the institutional environment (Kostova and Roth 2002). Regulative institutions directly relate to "rule-setting," "monitoring," and "sanctioning" activities in an organization (Scott 1998, 2001a, b) such as laws stating which behaviours are allowed (Palmer and Biggart 2002). For instance, the government can exert coercive pressure by political laws and decrees through which different types of constraints are applied. Besides constraints, it can provide some form of assistance, but again conditioned upon compliance to a set of nationally defined rules of the game. According to this pillar, a coercive mechanism takes care of conformation to institutions. Coercive isomorphism results from external pressures and by cultural expectations in the society. According to DiMaggio and Powell (1991a, b) it is the response to "both formal and informal pressures exerted on organisations by other organisations upon which they are dependent and by cultural expectations in the society within which organisations function" (p. 66). Coercive isomorphism, which stems from political influence and the problem of legitimacy, consider in particular the form of regulatory or other authoritative imperatives. However, this is not the case for IR as at present, because even if an internationally accepted Framework exists, only South African listed companies provide an IR by law. In the absence of coercion, other pressures on organizational behaviour may lead to accounting change driving towards the adoption of IR.

The *normative* institutional pillar refers to values, beliefs, norms and assumptions existing in the institutional environment that capture prescriptive, evaluative and obligatory dimensions of social life and provides structures of acceptable behaviour (Scott 2001a, b; Kostova and Roth 2002; Palmer and Biggart 2002). Normative institutions encompass rules-of-thumb, standards, operating procedures, occupational standards and educational curricula, and are based on social interactions and obligatory parts of these interactions (Hoffman 1999; Wicks 2001). They comprise of values, which reflect the proper ways, and norms, which reflect ways that are supposed to be followed (Scott 1998, 2001a, b). Their ability to influence employees and firm behaviour derives from seeking out conformity, enforcing social obligation, social necessity, and shared understandings of what is proper in the organization (Wicks 2001; Palmer and Biggart 2002). According to this pillar, the second mechanism is normative isomorphism which is "associated with professionalization" (DiMaggio and Powell 1991a, b). Normative isomorphism "arises when professionals operating in organisations are subject to pressures to conform to a set of norms and rules developed by occupational/professional groups" (Abernethy and Chua 1996, p. 574). In other words, the source of isomorphic organisational change is normative and stems primarily from professionalization (DiMaggio and Powell 1991a, b). In this form of isomorphism, organisations feel obliged to adopt structures, systems and processes that have been advocated by dominant occupational and professional groups (Burns 2000). The normative mechanism involves multiple processes of professionalization encouraged, or not, by the government for adoption by local institutions through some of the key actors. Jensen and Berg (2012) neglect this kind of mechanism in the case of IR, claiming that "Normative pressure denotes the impact that educational or professional authorities exert by setting standards to legitimate organizational practices. As business schools have not yet adopted IR in their curricula, these pressures are also negligible" (p. 301). However, Wild and Van Staden (2013) consider a further institutional pillar that can be applied while discussing the adoption of IR, the mimetic isomorphism, which is part of the cognitive institutional pillar.

The *cognitive* institutional pillar refers to widely shared social knowledge and cognitive categories such as stereotypes and schemes that represent the models of "individual behaviour based on subjectively constructed rules and meanings that dictate appropriate thought, feeling and action" (Wicks 2001, p. 57). Cultural-cognitive elements are "the shared conceptions that constitute the nature of social reality and the frames through which meaning is made" (Wicks 2001, p. 57). Cognitive institutions embody symbols-words, signs, and gestures as well as cultural rules and frameworks that guide understanding of the nature of reality and the frames through which meaning is developed (Hoffman 1999). They are reproduced through mimetic processes and organizations and organizational members follow these cognitive institutions without any conscious thought (Zucker 1983; Palmer and Biggart 2002). For cultural-cognitive theorists, compliance with cognitive components of the institutional environment occurs in many circumstances because other types of behaviour are inconceivable and routines are followed because they are taken for granted as "the way we do these things" (Scott 2001b, p. 57). The basis for compliance for an institution is also "taking this for granted" and is spread through mimicking others. This is the third mechanism, mimetic isomorphism, which occurs when organisations face uncertainty and "model themselves on other organisations" (DiMaggio and Powell 1983, p. 151). Organisations tend to copy those organisations that are perceived, in the same organisational field, to be more legitimate or successful, or those outside their organisational field that are similar to themselves in complexity. Mimetic isomorphism functions under ambiguous goals or an uncertain environment. Scapens (1994) argues that mimetic behaviour has a conformity element, wherein organisations adopt contemporary practices to legitimise their structures, systems and processes by appearing to be in control. Thus, the mimetic pressures imposed by the governments can arise from the drive to reduce uncertainty. Through this type of pressure, the government can for instance, encourage multiple imitations of the role model actors. Further, Jensen and Berg (2012, p. 301) posit that "IR is too new and the number of organizations having adopted it is too low to cause such a bandwagon effect". Considering the introduction of IR practices, Wild and Van Staden (2013) stated that the progressive adoption of this comprehensive communication tool can be considered as driven by a perceived need to conform to wider industry norms regarded as best practice, thus exercising a mimetic pressure on organisations within certain industries to adopt IR.

Together, coercive, mimetic and normative institutional processes can contribute to an emergent norm regarding organisational structures and procedures and the implementation of reform such as in this study with the accrual accounting system and its implementation. DiMaggio and Powell (1991a, b) argue that coercive, mimetic and normative forces produce homogeneity within a certain organisational field. However, the same authors pointed out that it may not always be possible to distinguish between the three forms of isomorphic pressure, and in fact, two or more of these may be operating simultaneously making it nearly impossible to determine which of them was potent in all cases. Summarizing, in the above sections, it is argued that an institutional perspective integrating New Institutional Sociology and Old Institutional Economics expands the levels of analysis encompassing both extra (macro) and intra (micro) organizational factors and consequently enhances the understanding of the conceptualisation of organizations actions and practices in terms of management accounting change.

2.3 Management Accounting Change

Accounting change and especially management accounting change research has drawn the interest of various researchers for many decades (Napier 2006). It was the 1980s that saw the emergence of this debate about management accounting change (Hopper and Powel 1985; Johnson and Kaplan 1987; Hopwood 1987, 1988; Scapens 1990). Since Hopwood (1987, p. 207) stated that little was known about "the preconditions for such change, the change process or its organizational consequences" accounting change has become an increasingly popular subject of considerable research and debate in management accounting literature. According to Burns and Scapens (2000) "Management accounting change has become a topic of much debate in recent years. Whether management accounting has not changed, has changed, or should change, have all been discussed" (p. 3).

This is not surprising, as change has been considered as being directly related to the organizational culture of the "New Economy", which is characterized by innovation, fast-paced operations, informal practices and the entrepreneurial spirit of risk investment. Therefore, many organizations have been experiencing significant changes in their organisational designs, competitive environments and information technologies which have highlighted the need for management accounting change (Bjøornenak and Olson 1999; Burns and Vaivio 2001). These changes ranged from minor modifications in existing management accounting systems which have been continuously to be used (Burns and Yazdifar 2001) to complete replacements or significant changes in management accounting systems and practices (Laitinen 2001; Sulaiman and Mitchell 2005).

As a result, there has been an increase in the number of empirical research studies interested in examining management accounting change in practice, although it has been argued that the nature of change is often taken for granted and its definition is avoided by researchers (Quattrone and Hopper 2001).

Furthermore, several studies have explored changes in management accounting practices and the role of accounting systems within the historical context of management accounting across organisations and public sector or the diffusion of new management accounting techniques (Lapsley and Wright 2004; Ax and Bjørnenak 2005; Fujimura 2007). In practice, both the rate of implementation and the degree of success of these new accounting techniques and systems have been variable (Kasurinen 2002). These empirical research studies have been conducted across many different business sectors and different national settings, and have adopted a multitude of research perspectives and methods. Many studies have been conducted in an attempt to understand why changes in management accounting practices actually occur (Scapens 1994; Anderson 1995; Abernethy and Chua 1996; Granlund and Lukka 1998; Burns and Scapens 2000; Granlund 2001; Soin et al. 2002; Guerreiro et al. 2006; Spraakman 2006). For example the drivers and correlates of accounting change (Anderson 1995; Libby and Waterhouse 1996; Gosselin 1997) have been examined as well as the conditions for the possibility for change and the influence of institutionalised elements on accounting change (Abernethy and Chua 1996; Burns and Scapens 2000). Several studies have proposed and/or adapted various conceptual frameworks, some from outside the accounting area, in order to explain how these changes have taken place in an effort to address a number of issues, including the management of the process of change and resistance to accounting change (Cooper 1990; Innes and Mitchell 1990a, b; Pettigrew et al. 1992; Scapens and Roberts 1993; Argyris and Kaplan 1994; Covaleski et al. 1996; Briers and Chua 2001; Quattrone and Hopper 2001; Guerreiro et al. 2004; Scapens 2006). Further, studies have confirmed that the circumstances of management accounting change can be both varied and complex by attributing importance to concepts such as trust, power and organizational politics (Burns 2000; Tomkins 2001). However, there is the view that less attention has been paid by researchers to the management accounting change process. It is supported that limited research has been conducted to understanding the process of management accounting systems and practices emergency or failure through time (Burns and Scapens 2000). In accordance with Stubbs and Higgins (2014), research in this area is ground on the idea that there is a need to promote a deep understanding of internal mechanisms employed by early adopters of IR, or to detect the extent to which IR is stimulating innovative disclosure mechanism. Thus, the constituents of management accounting change are discussed hereafter.

2.3.1 The Nature of Management Accounting Change

Much has been written on the changing nature of management accounting practice. It is broadly argued that the nature of change is often taken for granted and its definition is avoided by researchers (Burns and Vaivio 2001; Quattrone and Hopper 2001).

Management accounting change has been explored by various researchers via the employment of numerous approaches. Both interpretive and critical approaches as well as mainstream accounting approaches have been debated and formed theoretical frameworks to support management accounting research. Mainstream accounting researchers have not been particularly interested with the operational context of accounting, and accounting change has been viewed as an outcome of rational behaviour. With regard to mainstream approach, change has been best described with relevance to ideal accounting configurations instead of being explored via the complicated dynamics of change over time (Burns 2000). Contradictory, the interpretive and critical approaches have been considered management accounting change in its real life context such as organizational, cultural and social context. According to the interpretive and critical accounting approach, management accounting practices have been viewed as social practices and it is accepted that they are socially constructed implying thus the key role of social actors being involved in the management accounting process (Ryan et al. 2002). In this vein, a wide range of social theories have constituted a solid base for accounting researchers towards examining the process of accounting change in an organisational context such as the institutional framework that was broadly used lately (Scapens 1994; Burns and Scapens 2000; Moll et al. 2006; Ribeiro and Scapens 2006). According to Moll et al. (2006) an increasing number of organisational researchers who seek to understand why and how accounting has come thus far, have adopted institutional perspectives in order to conceptualise and explain management accounting change. More recently, the prominent role that institutional theories have taken in studying management accounting and accounting change has also been demonstrated by many researchers who have been concerned with the social and institutional dimensions of the organisational environments at the macro and micro levels (Moll et al. 2006; Ribeiro and Scapens 2006; Dragu and Tiron-Tudor 2013). According to Wickramasinghe and Alawattege (2007, p. 427), since the 1990s institutional theory "has become one of the popular theoretical frameworks in management accounting studies" and its main aim is to provide "an alternative framework with a sociological flavour". It is broadly accepted that institutional theory suggests the introduction of new accounting techniques in response to external environment changes legitimising thus organizational operations and securing organizational survival and stability (Scapens 1994; Burns and Scapens 2000; Ribeiro and Scapens 2006). Institutional theory considers management accounting to be an institution within the organization and perceives it as a widely taken for granted routine that embeds established and organisation wide accepted habits (Guerreiro et al. 2006). From an institutional theory perspective, Burns and Scapens (2000) have conceptualized management accounting change as change in organizational rules and routines. It is through the process of change and its institutionalization that management accounting, over a specific time horizon, may reflect the established rules and routines in an organisation as "taken-for-granted" ways of thinking and acting (Burns and Scapens 2000; Sulaiman and Mitchell 2005). Therefore, from the preceding discussion it can be derived that the adoption of an institutional theory perspective can constitute an alternative theoretical framework in explaining and interpreting change in management accounting and change also experienced in specific setting such as IR.

The debate over the changing nature of management accounting has been supported by a wide array of research, whose findings are not uniform and, sometimes, contradictory (Burns et al. 1999, 2003; Buscoet al. 2006; Wanderley et al. 2011). On the one hand, management accounting change can be understood as the introduction of new management accounting techniques (Baker and Bettner 1997; Hopper et al. 2001; Wanderley et al. 2011). On the other hand, management accounting change can be understood as the process of change in the manner in which traditional and/or new techniques are actually being used. Therefore management accounting changes occur with the creation and introduction of new techniques or with changes in the way managers use management accounting information generated by traditional systems (Wanderley et al. 2011). Wickramasinghe and Alawattege (2007) suggest change in management accounting as a learning methodology to understand how environmental factors shape the internal process within an organization.

According to learning methodology, the process of change reflects on the question of how management accounting techniques emerge, evolve and transform when new demands from the changing environment are in place. Management accounting change can be reflected in recent developments in three major areas: cost management, strategic management and management accounting in new organisations. It is considered as a shift from mechanistic to post-mechanistic approaches of management accounting.

By the 1990s, a stream of technical innovations were apparent and descriptions of their practical implementation were widespread, e.g. quality costing (Clark 1985), Activity Based Costing (Innes and Mitchell 1990a; Granlund and Lukka 1998; Sharman 2003; Kaplan and Anderson 2004), life cycle costing (Shields and Young 1991), throughput accounting (Darlington et al. 1992), Activity Based Cost management (Friedman and Lyne 1995), target costing (Dutton and Ferguson 1996), functional cost analysis (Yoshikawa et al. 1995), strategic management accounting (Dixon and Smith 1993; Coad 1996; Dixon 1998; Guilding et al. 2000; Lord 2007), shareholder value techniques (May and Bryan 1999; McLaren 1999) and the balanced scorecard (Kaplan and Norton 1992, 1996; Johnson 1998; Kasurinen 2002; Huang 2009). An increasing volume of case study research has provided further, more detailed evidence for the contemporary existence and nature of management accounting change. Cases, through their descriptive detail of management accounting change, have confirmed the great variety of forms through which change could take in practice. For example, Innes and Mitchell (1990b) found, in a series of high-tech company cases, a set of technical changes ranging from the replacement of management accounting techniques to their modification and extension. Amat et al. (1994) and Vaivio (1999) provided instances of change involving the supplementation of information in existing performance measurement packages. Kaplan (1986) and Granlund (2001) recounted changes concerning the alteration of the operation of ongoing cost systems. Shank (1996) and Jones and Dugdale (1998) observed the replacement of management decision support systems with new techniques. Wallander (1999) provided that management accounting change could also involve the abandonment of a technique, in this case traditional budgeting. Finally, Anderson and Young (2001) chronicled the "patchwork" variation of the technical nature of Activity Based Costing implementation across the production plants of two automobile producers. In these corporations change varied from comprehensive costing system replacement to tentative, partial and temporary change of a more modificatory type.

Case study research has also revealed some other dimensions of management accounting change. First, changes can be of different levels of importance and indeed the same type of change can be viewed differently, in this respect, in different organizations and by different parties to the change (Friedman and Lyne 1995; Innes and Norris 1997). Second, the level of success is another factor distinguishing change. This can range from failure to the achievement of different degrees of success (Cobb et al. 1992; Malmi 1997; Friedman and Lyne 1999). Other survey-based analyses have had a focus which has been extended beyond the adoption of new high profile techniques to consider the volume and prediction of management accounting change per se (Libby and Waterhouse 1996; Williams and Seaman 2001). Case studies have also been conducted to investigate how IR could help towards organizational change (Frías-Aceituno et al. 2013; Rowbottom and Locke 2016) routed on the first premises made by Eccles and Krzus (2010). Moreover Stubbs and Higgins (2014) conducted an exploratory study involving 15 organizations in Australia studying the internal mechanisms employed by early adopters of IR, elaborating on Laughlin's (1991) model of organisational change. As things stand, further consideration on the process of change and connection with the adoption of IR would be beneficial in order to gain a deeper understanding of the development of IR.

2.3.2 Understanding the Process of Change

Some extant accounting research has sought to reveal the constellation of elements conditioning accounting change. Historical studies have narrated complex configurations of socio-historical influences that create the conditions of possibility for accounting change including seemingly distant and global social discourses, such as those relating to efficiency or economic growth (Hopwood 1987; Miller 1991; Bhimani 1993). Collectively, research concerning the preconditions of accounting change affords an appreciation of the complex situations from which accounting change may emerge, and the multiple contextual elements constraining and/or enabling such change.

Given the fact that many entities both in the private and the public domains have experienced significant changes in their business environment, with advances in information technology, new management strategies, and a greater focus on quality and customer services, many relevant management accounting studies have highlighted the significant changes in these operating environments (Innes and Mitchell 1995; Kaplan and Norton 1996; Scapens 1999; Burns and Vaivio 2001; Hussain and Hoque 2002). These changes have influenced the choice of which management accounting systems and techniques would be most effective and have engendered the organization to reconsider its design and strategy in maintaining and/or improving performance (Baines and Langfield-Smith 2003; Choe 2004; Waldron 2005). In order to understand how different factors combine and interact to provide "real life" circumstances which either result, or do not result, in accounting change, a strand of studies has analysed the influencing factors in the process of management accounting change. Such studies have examined aspects of organisational design (Baines and Langfield-Smith 2003), organisational structure (Anderson 1995; Gosselin 1997) and corporate strategy (Shields 1995; Gosselin 1997; Baines and Langfield-Smith 2003). Further, certain organisational characteristics have proved to be preconditions for accounting change, such as: the presence of change facilitators (Innes and Mitchell 1990a, b), individual actor and task characteristics (Anderson 1995), qualities of accounting or manufacturing technologies (Innes and Mitchell 1990a, b; Baines and Langfield-Smith 2003), catalysts and motivators of change (Innes and Mitchell 1990a, b; Laitinen 2001), capacity for change (Libby and Waterhouse 1996) and top management support, linkage to performance evaluation and compensation, training and resource adequacy (Shields 1995).

Innes and Mitchell (1990a, b) analysed the factors influencing management accounting change and develop a threefold classification for describing the forces that exert pressure on organizations for change. The factors that correspond to a specific set of circumstances which affects management accounting change are termed as motivators, catalyst and facilitators. The interaction between these variables promotes change not only in management accounting but also other related disciplines (Innes and Mitchell 1990a, b; Laitinen 2006). *Motivators* are the factors that influence the observed changes in a general manner and relate to the level of competition in the market, the organisational structure, the production technology, the product cost structure and the length of the product life cycle. *Facilitators* are those factors that affect the success of accounting change such as accounting staff resources, computing resources and the degree of autonomy from the parent company. *Catalysts* are the factors that are directly associated with the change and the occurrence of which corresponds closely to the timing of change. The authors (Innes and Mitchell 1990a, b) considered that accounting change could occur through the interaction of these three types of factors. The motivators and catalysts act positively to generate change but can only become effective when suitable facilitating conditions exist. Innes and Mitchell (1990a, b) claimed that factors for accounting change are mainly focused on driving change and lacks explanation on how the process of accounting change occurs within an organisation.

Laitinen (2006), on the other hand, used four categories of factors to explain management accounting change i.e. organizational, financial, motivational factors and management tools. Changes in environment and technology are used as motivational factors in explaining management accounting change and changes in organizational factors, i.e., structure and strategy. Besides that, organizational structure and strategy have been considered as contextual factors inside the firm that may have a connection with change in management accounting (Moores and Yuen 2001).

Financial factors are used as outcomes of management accounting and organizational change. Granlund (2001) suggested that low financial performance might put economic pressure on the firm to change its management accounting systems to increase performance. Baines and Langfield-Smith (2003) suggested that if management accounting change pairs with a greater reliance on accounting information, it might result in improved performance. Thus, financial performance might be an antecedent or an outcome factor of management accounting change.

Scholarly work has observed the effect of institutional influences on change agendas as well; these could affect change through attempts to legitimise actions and demonstrate conformance with institutionalised rules and expectations (Covaleski et al. 1993). An organisation's institutional environment also influences the relative importance and role of new accounting practices in an organisation's "control mix" (Abernethy and Chua 1996). Covaleski et al. (1993) and Amat et al. (1994) argued that interactions and relative power between individual entities and their institutional environment should be investigated when considering the influence of institutional factors on accounting change.

There is also an extant literature exploring the processes of accounting change. The notion of "translation" is drawn upon in these studies to reflect the ways in which partisan interests are connected to diverse elements and funnelled through "obligatory passage points" (Miller 1991; Chua 1995). Further, various types of "boundary objects" have been observed to mediate and tie together diverse interests within networks, facilitating the process of accounting change (Briers and Chua 2001). Other work in relation to the processes of change has sought to examine the diffusion of accounting technologies. For example, Malmi (1999) examined the drivers of Activity Based Costing diffusion via several surveys of Finnish companies and found that the drivers of diffusion alter during the course of the diffusion lifecycle. Perera et al. (2003) also provided an account of diffusion with respect to transfer pricing at an Australian government trading enterprise. In this account, Perera et al. (2003) showed the importance of considering "secondary stage adoption" of organisational values, norms and previous experiences in understanding the trajectory of accounting diffusion.

Further studies examine the mobilisation of resistance in change processes. Resistance is seen to emanate from diverse origins and be rooted in a range of established organisational contingencies and historical legacies (Scapens and Roberts 1993; Malmi 1997). Such contingencies and legacies create inertial forces that counter change agendas (Granlund 2001). Studies have also characterised the enactment of resistance, identifying specific strategies that may be employed by professional groups to resist change. For example, in studies of accounting change in the British medical sector, it has been argued that the construction of "absorber groups" has contributed to the resistance of change by medical professionals (Laughlin et al. 1994; Broadbent and Laughlin 1998). These buffer groups of individuals were perceived to facilitate resistance by shielding the day-to-day practices of medical professionals from managerial incursions precipitated by accounting change. In summary, there has been a concerted research agenda to map the politics of change, factors influencing and shaping the trajectory of change, sites of resistance and the importance of influential agents and supporting elements in change processes.

Cobb et al. (1995) carried out a longitudinal case study to study management accounting change examining factors that hinder, delay or prevent change, i.e. the barriers to change. Examples of barriers have been indicated such as the changing priorities, accounting staff turnover and staff attitudes towards change. Several other factors have also been identified to influence the process of change within organizations, i.e. leadership and the influence of individuals and momentum for change, which is associated with the expectation of continuing change. In this study, motivators, catalysts, facilitators, leaders and momentum are collectively defined as advancing forces of change. Moreover, advancing forces and barriers are referred to as influencing forces of change. Cobb et al. (1995) explain that change can occur through the people within the organisation in relation to their need for information and their attitudes towards the change process.

Kasurinen (2002) in an effort to build on previous studies identified barriers to change. He claimed that motivators, catalysts and facilitators may be necessary to create a potential for change, but action by individuals is needed to overcome the barriers to change. Otherwise, the change initiative would be deflected by the barriers. On the other hand, change will not occur without commitment through the management process. Kasurinen (2002) suggested that the role of the barriers and of the influencing forces in the change process would be more easily recognized in a real-life organization, particularly if investigated at the early stages of a project. This consideration can be applied also in the case of IR: as discussed later on in depth, the preparation of IR requires the adoption of the "integrated thinking" which will result only by a process of management change. Moreover, considering that the role of accounting as a mediating practice, suitable to link up different actors with a common narrative and able to support a network of relations within and beyond the boundaries of the enterprise (Miller and Power 2013), the IR assumes nowadays a pivotal role both in changing management practices and in promoting different relations with a large plethora of stakeholders.

Christensen (2002) investigated the process of accounting change in the New South Wales State Government of Australia. Christensen (2002) focused on the history of the reform process and emphasized on the key actors of change identifying three groups of key actors: promoters of change, producers of information and users of information. Change could be promoted by people and organisations with a vested interest in wanting change, and it can be stimulated by the producers of information such as public servants in central agencies and government agency managers. Further, change could be stimulated by the users of information such as the politicians holding responsibility for individual portfolios or whole-of-government, as well as Opposition politicians and Parliamentary adjuncts. However, despite the desire for change, there can be implementation barriers, such as characteristics of the public sector itself and its accounting system that can restrict the options available to implement change.

2.3.3 The Notion of Change

Organizations have been defined as social structures that are created by individuals aiming to support collaborative pursuit of specified goals (Scott 2003). Organisations vary in terms of sizes and shapes, but, generally, every organisation has structure, a set of goals, technologies, participants, and physical limits that shape and constrain actions (Fligstein 1991; Scott 2003). The underlying assumption is that organisations can respond to changes in their environment because they are open systems (Lawrence and Lorsch 1986; Scott 2003). Furthermore, even though organisations may be confronted with the same or similar institutional environments, not all experience these influences the same way or respond in the same way (Scott 2001b). This implies that organisations are, at least to some extent, responsive to their institutional environment and influenced by this changing environment, and respond to these changes in one way or another. Meyer and Scott (1994, p. 210) viewed organizations as particularly affected by a changing environment, and stated that "… we see local organisation structures as embedded in a wider organisational system, and much affected by its properties". Although, it is important to know that organisations can respond to their environment, it is equally important to know how they might respond. Although the successful management of change is accepted as a necessity in order to survive and succeed in the highly competitive and continuously evolving environment of today, Balogun and Hailey (2004) reported a failure rate of around 70 % of all change programmes initiated. There is evidence that despite the efforts of understanding change better and learning from experience, change implementation in organisations still faces many problems. Elements such as the inability of managers to establish a sense of urgency for change, the wrong implementation of programs related to timing or to the structure of the objectives and the limited authority of leaders have been considered as causes of change failure (Beer et al. 1990; Pfeffer 1992; Kotter 1996). It may be suggested that the failure of change implementation implies a fundamental lack of a valid framework of change implementation and management as what is currently available to academics and practitioners is a wide range of contradictory and confusing theories and approaches (Burnes 2004). Thus, given the premise that change is unavoidable, the only rational solution is to learn more about what creates successful change, and to search for ways to manage change in a manner that best serves the interests of the organisation. When organizations respond to challenges by embarking on a change management path, they are faced with choices of which one of the management methods, techniques, and systems would be most effective (Kotter 1996; Waldron 2005). Furthermore, to explain the organizational and human response to change and the determinants of a successful change process it is needed to understand the notion and the nature of change and the why and how the change is affected by the dynamics of the change process.

According to Quattrone and Hopper (2001, p. 404) "little is known about what change is". However, there seems to be an agreement on two important issues. Firstly, it is agreed that the pace of change has never been greater than in the current business environment (Balogun and Hailey 2004; Burnes 2004; Carnall 2003; Kotter 1996; Luecke 2003). Secondly, there is a consensus that change being triggered by internal or external factors affects all the different kinds of organizations (Carnall 2003; Luecke 2003; Balogun and Hailey 2004; Burnes 2004). Change has become a broadly accepted paradox through the statement of the Greek philosopher Heraclitus that "change is the only constant". Change is an ever-present feature of organisational life, both at an operational and strategic level (Burnes 2004). Weber and Weber (2001) supported that many organizations have recognized that change is an organizational good which enhances the productiveness and success of the organization. Described simply, a change is a shift in some condition or situation from its present state to a new and different state (French and Bell 1999; Mecca 2004). From this perspective, change involves a deliberative approach to revising and replacing what is currently in place. The word "change" is often used to refer both to a shift that occurs in the organization's external environment, as well as the changes that occur inside of the organization in response to shifts in its external environment.

Literature on organizational change has described and defined change in several ways, either from an organizational or an individual perspective. Change has often been viewed as being related to the operations and structures of organisations. Lewin (1947, 1951) is one of the early researchers in the area of change, particularly with his examination of the social responses to change and the psychological processes experienced by those involved with change. Lewin (1947, 1951) depicted change as being a dynamic process between the driving forces of change and the competing forces of resistance and defined organizational change as an event that is frozen, unfrozen, and refrozen (Lewin 1951). Organizational change was expressed as "an empirical observation of difference in form, quality, or state over time in an organizational entity. The entity may be an individual's job, a work group, an organizational strategy, a program, a product, or the overall organization" (Van de Ven and Poole 1995, p. 512).

Ford and Ford (1995, p. 543) described change as "the difference(s) between two (or more) successive conditions, states, or moments of time". It has also been claimed by Schalk et al. (1998, p. 157) that change is "the deliberate introduction of novel ways of thinking, acting and operating within an organisation as a way of surviving or accomplishing certain organisational goals". These definitions consider change as a planned process that occurs within an organization without referring to triggers leading to change or change management. More recently, Lines (2005, p. 10) also viewed change as a planned process and focused on the organizational outcomes describing the process of change as "a deliberately planned change in an organisation's formal structure, systems, processes or product-market domain intended to improve the attainment of one or more organisational objectives".

However, according to Grover et al. (1995) change is, at best, "complex and not easily accomplished, involving the manipulation of interactive relationships among such organisational subcomponents as management, people, structure, technology and rewards".

Change is referred to as the effective implementation of planned change through a sequence of activities, processes and leadership that produces organisational improvements to enhance economic potential and the creation of competitive advantage (Cummings and Worley 2001). Change is also characterized as an effort that consists of actual physical changes to operations and different emotional stimulation, is painful in the workplace, moving from what is certain and known to the otherwise (Bernerth 2004). Since the need for change often is unpredictable, it tends to be reactive, discontinuous, ad hoc and often triggered by situations of organisational crisis (Luecke 2003; Burnes 2004; De Wit and Meyer 2005). There is the common view that change cannot be understood as a sequence of events occurring within a specified time period (Dawson 1994; Greenwood and Hinnings 1996). This infers that a processual approach should be used to understand why and how change is developed in the subject organisation.

2.3.4 *Why and When Change?*

Triggers of change "are the factors which may conspire to initiate change both internally and externally regardless of whether these are seen as needs, opportunities or threats" (Grundy 1993). Organisational change literature suggests organisations change for many reasons. For example, change can occur as a response to external pressures i.e., market pressures, government laws and regulations, technological advances, competitors, customer expectations, social and political changes or internal pressures e.g., power dynamics, new strategic directions of the organisation, obsolete services and products, changing size and complexity of the organization and an increasingly diverse workforce (George et al. 2002; Kieffer 2005). Further, it is suggested that organisations do not always wait for legitimacy to be conferred; rather, they can make a conscious choice in order to be perceived as legitimate. It is also contended that there may be multiple pressures for change that may be interdependent. As an example Dawson (1994, p. 14) wrote, "a push for change in technology may result from competitive pressures or from the exposure of local engineering personnel of the benefits of new developments in capital equipment".

Greenberg and Baron (1993) described organisational change with some examples (Table 2.1). Change is characterized as planned and deliberate or unplanned and random due to external or internal changes.

The planned approach emphasises the importance of understanding the different states, which an organisation will have to go through in order to move from an unsatisfactory state to an identified desired state (Elrod II and Tippett 2002). Planned change concerns the deliberate and concerted effort for new conditions and circumstances to be established. Unplanned change is not consciously produced. It is produced rather through side effects, through some subsidiary event or secondary effect or even unexpected consequences of action (Ford and Ford 1995; April 1999). The planned approach to change was initiated by Lewin (1946) and since

Table 2.1 Examples of organisational change (adapted from Greenberg and Baron 1993, p. 624)

	Planned change	Unplanned change
Internal change	• Changes in products or services • Changes in administrative systems	• Changing employee demographics • Performance gaps
External change	• Introduction of new technologies • Advances in information processing and communication	• Government regulations • External competition

then a large amount of research has been conducted around the planned change approach, as it was subscribed to by Lewin (Cummings and Worley 2001). However, there is the view that organisations change mainly due to external pressure rather than an internal desire to change (Goodstein and Burke 1997). Thus, although the planned approach to change is long established and held to be highly effective (Bamford and Forrester 2003; Burnes 2004), it has come under increasing criticism since the early 1980s (Kanter et al. 1992; Burnes 1996). Criticism was mainly exercised by the advocates of the emergent approach. They suggested that the planned approach viewed organizations operating under constant conditions and moving in a pre-planned manner from one state to another new one (Bamford and Forrester 2003). They also claimed that the change planned approach focused mainly on small scale change with a common agreement questioning thus its applicability in rapid and major change needed in an increasingly rapid changing business environment and that the emergent approach suggests that change be driven from the bottom-up rather than the top-down (Bamford and Forrester 2003; Burnes 1996, 2004). The emergent approach stresses the unpredictable nature of change, and views change as a process of learning. According to the advocates of the emergent approach to change it is the uncertainty of both the external and internal environment that makes this approach more pertinent than the planned approach (Bamford and Forrester 2003). To cope with the complexity and uncertainty of the environment it is suggested that organisations need to become open learning systems where strategy development and change emerges from the way a company as a whole acquires, interprets and processes information about the environment (Dunphy and Stace 1993). The approach stresses a promotion of "extensive and in-depth understanding of strategy, structure, systems, people, style and culture, and how these can function either as sources of inertia that can block change, or alternatively, as levers to encourage an effective change process" (Burnes 1996, p. 14).

It could, therefore, be suggested that the emergent approach to change is more concerned with change readiness and facilitating change than to provide specific pre-planned steps for each change project and initiative. As the emergent approach to change is relatively new compared to the planned approach, it is argued that it still lacks coherence and a diversity of techniques (Wilson 1992; Bamford and Forrester 2003). However, according to Burnes (1996) the general applicability and validity of the emergent approach to organisational change depends on whether or not it is believed that organisations operate in dynamic and unpredictable environments to which they constantly have to adapt. As Burnes argues (1996, p. 14), "the emergent model is suitable for all organizations, all situations and at all times". Independently from whether the planned or emergent approach is viewed, as suitably concerned the change efforts organizations make in order to face changing environmental challenges, they do not guarantee the type of strategies and responses from organizations. According to Oliver (1991), organisational responses to institutional pressures "will vary from conforming to resistant, from passive to active, from preconscious to controlling, from impotent to influential, and from habitual to opportunistic, depending on the institutional pressures toward conformity that are exerted on organisations" (p. 151).

Scott pointed out different strategies and aspects followed by organizations at different rates (Scott 1998). Participants' key role is recognized as influencing the type of organizational response to changes, as "in order to make a decision to change an organisation, individuals must perceive a need and source for that change" (Fligstein 1991, p. 315). In the end, the adoption of new work practices or behaviours is more likely to be accepted if people affected by the change would perceive the related benefits.

Lapsley and Pettigrew (1994) discussed management accounting change in the public sector realm—and specifically in healthcare organizations—as a helpful approach to afford the complexity related to public sector organizations. In this kind of organization, characterized by ambiguity objectives, where output is often difficult to define and measure readily (Hofstede 1981), approaching innovative management accounting practice can be supportive for the success (and the flourishing) of the entity. Elaborating on the two models proposed by Pettigrew and Whipp (1993), Pettigrew et al. (1992) and Lapsley and Pettigrew (1994) focused on the 'why' and 'what' of change, encompassing both external and internal factors. Thus, a model of change, which includes economic, social and political events side by side with the factors characterising any single organization is discussed. The factors namely are identification of a high quality and coherent policy, availability of key people to lead the change, existence of long-term environmental pressures, presence of a supportive organizational culture, development of effective managerial and clinical relations, existence of cooperative inter-organizational networks, articulation of simple and clear goals, and stipulation of a change agenda and its locale. With regard to these internal factors, the authors consider how the needed changes are formulated, by whom and how the change effort itself is managed.

Based on the work of Lapsley and Pettigrew, Padovani et al. (2014) highlighted how these factors have to be managed as interlinked and mutually reinforcing loops. In addition, with respect to the inner context, the Padovani et al. model includes also 'receptive' and 'non-receptive' contexts for change. The former refers to organizations in which different actors favourable accept and/or promote the changes. The latter is related to organizations within which some parties oppose to change, creating thus barriers to its successful implementation.

Many change models have been promoted about a better understanding of change relating to organizations. Among the first ones published and also the most renowned and referred model of planned change is Lewin's (1951) three-phase process: *unfreezing* the old, *moving to new* and *refreezing* the new behaviour or situation. Lewin suggested that in order for change and new behaviour to be adopted successfully, the previous behaviour has to be discarded (Elrod and Tippett 2002; Burnes 2004). The first phase of *unfreezing*, preparing the climate for change, creates discomfort with the status quo and alters the present stable equilibrium which supports existing behaviours and attitudes. The *moving phase* involves evaluation and analysis, the design and implementation of a new dispensation developing thus new responses based on new information. The refreezing phase institutionalises the change by reinforcing the new equilibrium of the organisation at a different level through various mechanisms, for instance, performance management, training, entrenching of organisational values, and stabilize the change by introducing the new responses into the personalities of those concerned (Armstrong 2006). This model of change recognises the need of discarding old behaviour, structures, processes and culture before successfully adopting new approaches (Bamford and Forrester 2003). Lewin's three-step model is still considered to be one of the most accurate descriptions of how change occurs, describing change as a series of transitions between different states. According to the model, no change will occur unless unfreezing the system, and no change will last unless the refreezing the system. According to Burnes (2004) Lewin's model was implied group dynamics and suggested how individuals will usually go along with the group norm. Armstrong (2006) also noted that Lewin's model suggested a "field force analyses" by analysing and assessing the restraining or driving forces of change and taking actions to increase or decrease respectively the driving or restraining forces. Lewin's model has been criticised for being too simplistic and thus, not offering practical enough information for carrying out change in practice (Kanter et al. 1992; Elrod and Tippett 2002).

Several authors have, therefore, developed Lewin's work in an attempt to make it more practical (Bamford and Forrester 2003). For example, Bullock and Batten (1985) developed a four-phase model of planned change that contains phases of exploration, planning, action and integration. The model concerns both the processes of change and describes the methods employed to move an organisation from one state to another, and the phases of change and describes the stages an organisation must go through to achieve successful change implementation. Robertson and Seneviratne (1995) added changes in technology and physical setting to the ways change can be accomplished. The proposed model illustrates three phases. First, planned interventions create changes in the organization work setting. These changes in the work setting lead to behavioural changes which, finally, impact organizational performance and individual development considering them as the desired organizational outcomes. According to Grover et al. (1995) change implementation revolves around activities pertaining to the initiation, adoption and institutionalisation of change. Initiation efforts include establishing a vision, aligning change efforts with the organisation's strategy, identifying opportunities, enabling IT systems, and so on. Adoption revolves around commitment and communication. It may therefore involve senior management's commitment to new values, mustering the required resources, and communication between management and employees with regard to the need for, scope of and commitment required for the project. This phase requires careful preparation in anticipation of organisation-wide radical change. Institutionalisation includes designing, installing and evaluating new business processes, structures and systems. Goodstein and Burke (1997) have also added more detailed phases and action into Lewin's model describing unfreezing phases such as top management changes, reduction of the levels of hierarchy, redefinition of the business and top management commitment and involvement. The moving phase contains empowering and participation of employees, supporting the change by support groups, new incentives and bonuses, intensive training according to the business strategy and values and management tools to support the change. The final phase of refreezing relates to continuous monitoring and feedback, promoting the new values, new performance appraisal system and use of task forces.

One of the most popular is Kotter's phase model (Table 2.2). Kotter (1995, 1996) studied over a hundred organisations having carried out a planned change effort and came up with eight most common mistakes causing programs to fail. However, he introduced methods for avoiding those mistakes and fatal errors by constructing an eight stage change process for implementing organisational transformation. He justified the eight step model by first claiming that all useful changes tend to be associated with a multistep process that creates enough power and motivation for overwhelming the sources of inertia.

Kotter stated that it is imperative to pay attention to all of the phases and depending on the nature of the change and the current state of the organisation, all successful change efforts go through all eight stages in his process (Kotter 1996). More recently, Kotter and Cohen (2002) suggested that large-scale organisational

Table 2.2 Kotter's eight step phase model (1995, 1996)

Kotter's eight step phase model	
1.	Establishing a sense of urgency, harnessing the external crises and opportunities facing an organization
2.	Creating the guiding coalition, engaging the participants within an organisation around change
3.	Developing a vision and strategy articulating the desired end result of the change process
4.	Communicating the change vision within the organisation through all available communication channels
5.	Generating short term wins and publicising the success of managing change
6.	Generating short term wins and publicising the success of managing change
7.	Consolidating gains and producing more change revising processes and operations that are inconsistent with the change vision
8.	Anchoring new approaches in the culture by articulating the change efforts with future organisational success

change efforts can only be successful if the following eight steps are handled well: increase urgency, building the guiding team, getting the vision right, communication for buy-in, empowering action, creation of short-term wins, sustaining the effort and making change stick. The above mentioned elements are all considered essential steps within a successful change initiative. Furthermore, Kotter (1995) reviewed the results derived from the incorrect order or wrong way the eight steps are followed. More recently, Armstrong (2006) building on Kotter's eight steps model, proposed enacting actions in each step, such as follows:

1. Establishing a sense of urgency by taken consideration of market and competitive realities and by identified and discussed crises or major opportunities.
2. Forming a powerful guiding coalition by assembling a group with enough power to lead the change effort and encouraging the group to work together as a team.
3. Creating a vision to help direct the change effort and in turn developing strategies for achieving that vision.
4. Communicating the vision using every vehicle possible to communicate the new vision and strategies and teaching new behaviours by the example of the guiding coalition.
5. Empowering others to act on the vision by getting rid of obstacles to change, changing systems or structures that seriously undermine the vision and encourage risk taking and non-traditional ideas, activities and actions.
6. Planning for and creating short-term wins, planning for visible performance improvement, creating those improvements and recognizing and rewarding employees involved in the improvements;
7. Consolidating improvements and producing still more change by using increased credibility to change systems, structures and polices that don't fit the vision, hiring, promoting and developing employees who can implement the vision and reinvigorating the process with new projects, themes and change agents.
8. Institutionalizing new approaches by articulating the connections between the new behaviours and corporate success and developing the means to ensure leadership development and succession (Armstrong 2006).

However, even change models have not survived without criticism. For instance, Kanter et al. (1992) argued that phase models may be just a little too simple. Cummings and Worley (1993) further addressed that another deficiency in planned change and phase models is that the picture they portray about change effort is misleading. They also noted that in practice even planned change is chaotic by nature, involving shifting goals, surprising events, and unexpected turnarounds. Furthermore, change and phase models have been typically characterised as a sequence of phases or activities needed to be carried out in a successful organisational change. Merely outlining some general steps, however, is not adequate and does not meet the challenge, namely offering information as to how different steps should be taken in different situations, surroundings and environments (Cummings and Worley 1993). The criticism on phase models is mainly focused on their oversimplifying nature and the lack of causality and clear contingency frameworks. Kotter (1996) also reminded that although different phases are described in a quite straightforward and simple way, they often overlap and thus the entire change effort increasingly resembles an evolving process rather than clearly phased progression. He further notes that it is not meaningful to draw a clear line between the phases separating the end of one step from the beginning of the next. Although Kotter stated that it is important to initiate action in the specific order described in his eight-stage model, many different stages may be under way at the same time. Still, he seriously pointed out, that both forgoing even a single step and failing to build a solid base for moving up in the process almost always creates problems (Kotter 1996).

2.4 Integrated Reporting: An Accounting Change Approach

Recently researchers have utilised various institutional theory strands with a clear aim towards gaining insights into the areas of organisational and management accounting change. More specifically, New Institutional Sociology and Old Institutional Economics have often dominated and advanced the study of management accounting and management accounting change aiming towards the investigation of the environmental and organisations' social and institutional dimensions. Both institutional perspectives embed into their analysis social dimensions such as culture and society, and they both focus in the way in which institutions shape organizations and the actions of organizational actors, and how new rules and institutions may emerge under institutional pressures. Despite striving towards the achievement of this aim, the convergence between both institutional strands has not proven its merit yet providing rather complementary insights. According to both of them, institutions organize action while they provide the definition of the behaviour and the appropriate actor relationships (Yazdifar 2003). However, New Institutional Sociology focuses on the external pressures exerted on organisations that shape them and impact on their structure and the way they are governed (Scapens 2006). On the other hand, Old Institutional Economics focuses on institutions that cultivate and shape the organizational actors thoughts and actions (Scapens 2006).

Mainly, by considering management accounting change, this study intends to verify, through a case-study on the progressive implementation of the IR, how the intra organizational dynamics play a key role in the evolution of management accounting change interacting with each other, and impacting on the overall result and success of the change process. This means, that even though the initial stage of motivating/encoding may be successfully activated, the successful progress of the process can fall in part or entirely in the next phase of managing/enacting or later on in the final stage of reproducing/institutionalizing.

The emergence of the need for change and the initial positive reaction of the staff involved with change under a strong coalition that will guide and support change is not enough to secure the successful progress of the change process. Managing the whole process has also demanded to be activated in a positive way such as top management commitment, communication, professional training and assistance of supporting systems developing thus new behaviours and securing the universal participation in the change process. Achieving successful change pre requires supporting participants to adjust to the continuously changing environment, keeping communication and maintaining the organization's vision clear during the change process while taking into consideration every member involved. Therefore, change is more likely to be successfully completed (Brisson-Banks 2010).

Finally, in reaching the final stage of the change process, there is a requirement for new practices to be enforced by continuous repetition, evaluation and rewarding, in order to be totally institutionalized and also unconsciously accepted and considered as routines on a daily basis and lead to the positive outcome of the accounting change process.

The above discussion highlights once more the complexity of the management accounting change process. This means that the relevant skills and expertise are needed to bring about the change to be successfully adopted in each phase of the change process. Therefore, this study hopefully contributes to the provision of knowledge related to the phenomenon of accounting change and allows for a deeper understanding of the management accounting change process in order for the phenomenon to be more efficiently managed by key organizational actors and managers of similar organizations. The case study proposed in the last chapter analyses the adoption of IR by looking at the undergoing management accounting change process in light of the model discussed by Armstrong (2006).

Grounding on the theories and the model discussed in this chapter, the case study proposed in the last chapter intends to grasp a useful "lesson to learn" for other entities located in the public sector realm, that intend to introduce IR.

References

Abdul Khalid SN (2000) An institutionalist study of resistance to management accounting change. Unpublished Ph.D. thesis, Manchester School of Accounting and Finance

Abernethy MA, Chua WF (1996) A field study of control systems "redesign": the impact of institutional processes on strategic choice. Contemp Account Res 13(2):569–606

Amat J, Carmona S, Roberts H (1994) Context and change in management accounting systems: a Spanish case study. Manag Acc Res 5(2):107–122

Anderson SW (1995) Framework for assessing cost management system changes: the case of activity-based costing implementation at General Motors 1986–1993. J Manag Acc Res 7 (1):1–51

Anderson SW, Young SM (2001) Implementing management innovations. Kluwer Academic Publishers, The Netherlands

April KA (1999) Leading through communication, conversation and dialogue. Leadersh Organ Dev J 20(5):231–242

Argyris C, Kaplan RS (1994) Implementing new knowledge: the case of activity-based costing. Acc Horiz 8(3):83

Armstrong M (2006) A Handbook of human resource management practice, 10th edn. Kogan Page, London

Ax C, Bjørnenak T (2005) Bundling and diffusion of management accounting innovations—The case of the balanced scorecard in Sweden. Manag Acc Res 16(1):1–20

Baines A, Langfield-Smith K (2003) Antecedents to management accounting change: a structural equation approach. Acc Organ Soc 28(7):675–698

Baker CR, Bettner M (1997) Interpretative and critical research in accounting: a commentary on its absence from mainstream accounting research. Crit Perspect Account 8(4):293 310

Balogun J, Hailey VH (2004) Exploring strategic change, 2nd edn. Prentice-Hall, Harlow

Bamford DR, Forrester PL (2003) Managing planned and emergent change within an operations management environment. Int J Oper Production Manag 23(5):546–564

Barley SR, Tolbert PS (1997) Institutionalization and structuration: Studying the links between action and institution. Organ Stud 18(1):93–117

Baxter J, Chua WF (2003) Alternative management accounting research—Whence and whither accounting. Organ Soc 28(2/3):97–126

Beer M, Eisenstat RA, Spector B (1990) Why change programs don't produce change. Harvard Bus Rev 68(6):158–166

Bernerth J (2004) Expanding our understanding of the change message. Hum Resour Dev Rev 3(1):36–52

Bhimani A (1993) Performance measures in UK manufacturing companies: The state of play. Manag Acc 71(11):20–22

Bjøornenak T, Olson O (1999) Unbundling management accounting innovations. Manag Acc Res 10(4):325–338

Boons F, Strannegård L (2000) Organizations coping with their natural environment: a laboratory for institutionalization? Int Stud Manag Organ 30(3):7–17

Briers M, Chua WF (2001) The role of actor-networks and boundary objects in management accounting change: a field study of an implementation of activity-based costing. Acc Organ Soc 26(3):237–269

Brignall S, Modell S (2000) An institutional perspective on performance measurement and management in the 'new public sector'. Manag Acc Res 11(3):281–306

Brisson-Banks CV (2010) Managing change and transitions: a comparison of different models and their commonalities. Libr Manag 31(4/5):241–252

Broadbent J, Guthrie J (1992) Changes in the public sector: A review of recent 'alternative' accounting research. Acc Auditing Accountability J 5(2):3–31

Broadbent J, Laughlin R (1998) Resisting the "new public management": absorption and absorbing groups in schools and GP practices in the UK. Acc Auditing Accountability J 11(4): 403–435

Brunsson N, Sahlin-Andersson K (2000) Constructing organizations: the example of public sector reform. Organ Stud 21(4):721–746

Bullock RJ, Batten D (1985) It's just a phase we're going through: a review and synthesis of OD phase analysis. Group Organ Manage 10(4):383–412

Burnes B (1996) No such thing as… a "one best way" to manage organizational change. Manag Decis 34(10):11–18

Burnes B (2004) Managing change: a strategic approach to organisational dynamics. Financial Times Prentice Hall, Harlow

Burns J (2000) The dynamics of accounting change inter-play between new practices, routines, institutions, power and politics. Acc Auditing Accountability J 13(5):566–596

Burns J (2001) Institutional theory in management accounting research: towards more pluralistic dialogue in conceptualizing management accounting change. MSA Dis.P
Burns J, Vaivio J (2001) Management accounting change. Manag Acc Res 12(4):389–402
Burns J, Scapens RW (2000) Conceptualizing management accounting change: an institutional framework. Manag Acc Res 11(1):3–25
Burns J, Yazdifar H (2001) Tricks or treats. Finan Manag 33–35
Burns J, Ezzamel M, Scapens RW (1999) Management accounting change in the UK. Manag Acc 77(3):28–30
Burns J, Ezzamel M, Scapens RW (2003) The challenge of management accounting change: behavioural and cultural aspects of change management. CIMA, Elsevier Ltd, Amsterdam
Busco C, Riccaboni A, Scapens RW (2006) Trust for accounting and accounting for trust. Manag Acc Res 17(1):11–41
Carnall C (2003) Managing change in organizations. Pearson Education Limited, Harlow
Carpenter VL, Feroz EH (2001) Institutional theory and accounting rule choice: an analysis of four us state governments' decisions to adopt generally accepted accounting principles. Acc Organ Soc 26(7):565–596
Carruthers BG (1995) Accounting, ambiguity, and the new institutionalism. Account Organ Soc 26:565–596
Choe JM (2004) The relationships among management accounting information, organizational learning and production performance. J Strateg Inf Syst 13(1):61–85
Christensen M (2002) Accrual accounting in the public sector: the case of the New South Wales government. Acc Hist 7(2):93–124
Chua WF (1995) Experts, networks and inscriptions in the fabrication of accounting images: a story of the representation of three public hospitals. Acc Organ Soc 20(2/3):111–145
Clark KB (1985) The interaction of design hierarchies and market concepts in technological evolution. Res Policy 14(5):235–251
Coad A (1996) Smart work and hard work: explicating a learning orientation in strategic management accounting. Manag Acc Res 7(4):387–408
Cobb I, Helliar C, Innes J (1995) Management accounting change in a bank. Manag Acc Res 6(2):155–175
Cobb P, Wood T, Yackel E, Perlwitz M (1992) A follow-up assessment of a second-grade problem-centered mathematics project. Educ Stud Math 23(5):483–504
Contrafatto M, Burns J (2013) Social and environmental accounting, organisational change and management accounting: a processual view. Manag Acc Res 24(4):349–365
Cooper DJ (1990) Critical accounts: reorientating accounting research. T Hopper (ed). Macmillan Press, London
Covaleski MA, Dirsmith MW, Michelman JE (1993) An institutional theory perspective on the DRG framework case-mix accounting systems and healthcare organizations. Acc Organ Soc 18 (1):65–80
Covaleski MA, Dirsmith MW, Samual S (1996) Managerial accounting research: the contributions of organizational and sociological theories. J Manag Acc Res 8:1–35
Cummings TG, Worley CG (1993) Organization development and change. West Publishing Company, Minneapolis
Cummings TG, Worley CG (2001) Organization development and change. Cengage learning, Stanford
Dacin MT, Goodstein J, Scott WR (2002) Institutional theory and institutional change: Introduction to the special research forum. Acad Manag J 45(1):43–56
Darlington J, Innes J, Mitchell F, Woodward J (1992) Throughput accounting: the garrett automotive experience. Manag Acc 73:23–80
Dawson C (1994) Human resource accounting: From prescription to description? Manag Decis 32(6):35–40
De Wit B, Meyer R (2005) Strategy synthesis: resolving strategy paradoxes to create competitive advantage. Thomson Learning, 2nd ed. London

DiMaggio PJ, Powell WW (1983) The iron cage revisited: Institutional isomorphism and collective rationality in organizational fields. Am Sociol Rev 48(2):147–160
DiMaggio PJ, Powell WW (1991a) The new institutionalism in organizational analysis. University of Chicago Press, Chicago
DiMaggio PJ, Powell WW (1991b) The iron cage revisited: institutional isomorphism and collective rationality in organisational fields. In: WW Powell, PJ DiMaggio (eds) The new institutionalism in organisational analysis. University of Chicago Press, Chicago, pp 63–82
Dillard JF, Rigsby JT, Goodman C (2004) The making and remaking of organization context: duality and the institutionalization process. Acc Auditing Accountability J 17(4):506–542
Dixon R (1998) Accounting for strategic management: a practical application. Long Range Plan 31 (2):272–279
Dixon R, Smith D (1993) Strategic management accounting. Omega 21(6):605–618
Djelic ML, Quack S (2003) Globalization and institutions: redefining the rules of the economic game. Edward Elgar, Cheltenham
Dragu IM, Tiron-Tudor A (2013) The integrated reporting initiative from an institutional perspective: emergent factors. Procedia-Social and Behavioral Sciences 92:275–279
Dugger W, Sherman H (1994) Comparison of institutionalism and Marxism. J Econ 28(1):101–128
Dunphy D, Stace D (1993) The strategic management of corporate change. Hum Relat 46(8):16–19
Dutton JJ, Ferguson M (1996) Target costing at texas instruments. J Cost Manag 33–38
Eccles RG, Krzus MP (2010) One Report. Integrated reporting for a sustainable society. Wiley, USA
Eggertsson T (1996) A note on the economics of institutions. In: Alston LJ, Eggertsson T, North DC (eds) Empirical studies in institutional change. Cambridge University Press, Cambridge, pp 6–24
Elrod PDII, Tippett DD (2002) The "Death Valley" of change. J Organ Change Manag 15(3):273–291
Feldman MS (2000) Organizational routines as a source of continuous change. Organ Sci 11(6)
Feldman MS, Pentland BT (2003) Reconceptualizing organizational routines as a source of flexibility and change. Adm Sci Q 48(1):94–118
Fligstein N (1991) The structural transformation of American industry: an institutional account of the causes of diversification I the largest firms, 1919–1979. In: Powell W, DiMaggio P (eds) The new institutionalism in organizational analysis. University of Chicago Press, Chicago, pp 311–336
Ford JD, Ford LW (1995) The role of conversations in producing intentional change in organizations. Acad Manag Rev 20(3):541–570
Foster BP, Ward TJ (1994) The theory of perpetual management accounting innovation lag in hierarchical organizations. Acc Organ Soc 19(4–5):401–411
French WL, Bell CH (1999) Organization development, 6th edn. Prentice Hall, Englewood Cliffs
Frías-Aceituno JV, Rodríguez-Ariza L, García-Sánchez IM (2013) Is integrated reporting determined by a country's legal system? An exploratory study. J Clean Prod 44:45–55
Friedman AL, Lyne SR (1995) Activity-based techniques. Chartered Institute of Management Accountants
Friedma, AL, Lyne SR (1999) Success and failure of activity-based techniques: a long-term perspective. Chartered Institute of Management Accountants
Fujimura D (2007) Lyman Mills and its encounter with public accountants. Inventory Costing Circa 19 20. Acc Historians J 34 (2):169–200
George JM, Jones GR, Sharbrough WC (2002) Understanding and managing organizational behavior. Prentice Hall, Upper Saddle River
Goodstein LD, Burke WW (1997) Creating successful organization change. In: Carnall CA (ed) Strategic change. Butterworths-Heinemann, Oxford, pp 158–173
Gosselin M (1997) The effect of strategy and organisational structure on the adoption and implementation of activity-based costing. Acc Organ Soc 22(2):105–122

Granlund M (2001) Towards explaining stability in and around management accounting systems. Manag Acc Res 12(2):141–166
Granlund M, Lukka K (1998) It's a small world of management accounting practices. J Manag Acc Res 10:154–179
Greenberg J, Baron RA (1993) Behavior in organizations: understanding and managing the human side of work. Allyn and Bacon, Greenberg
Greenwood R, Hinnings CR (1996) Understanding radical organizational change: bringing together the old and the new institutionalism. Acad Manag Rev 21(4):1022–1054
Grover V, Teng J, Fiedler K (1995) The implementation of business process reengineering. J Manag Inf Syst 12(1):109–44
Grundy T (1993) Putting value on a strategy. Long Range Plan 26(3):87–94
Guerreiro R, Pereira CA, Frezatti F (2006) Evaluating management accounting change according to the institutional theory approach: a case study of a Brazilian bank. J Acc Organ Change 2 (3):196–228
Guerreiro R, Casado T, Bio SR (2004) Some reflections on the archetypes in cost accounting: an exploratory study. J Appl Manag Acc Res 2(1):41–54
Guilding C, Cravens KS, Tayles M (2000) An international comparison of strategic management accounting practices. Manag Acc Res 11:113–135
Hannan MT, Freeman J (1984) Structural inertia and organizational change. Am Sociol Rev 49(2):149–164
Hannan MT, Freeman J (1977) The population ecology of organizations. Am J Sociol 82(5):9 29–964
Hannan MT, Freeman J (1989) Organizations and social structure. Organ Ecol 3–27
Hodgson G (1993) Institutional economics: surveying the old and the new. Metroeconomica 44: 1–28
Hodgson G (1998) The approach of institutional economics. J Econ Lit 26:166–192
Hodgson G (2007) Institutions and individuals: interaction and evolution. Organ Stud 28(1): 95–116
Hodgson G (2008) The concept of a routine. In: Becker M (ed) Handbook of organizational routines. Edward Elgar, Cheltenham, pp 15–28
Hoffman AJ (1999) Institutional evolution and change: environmentalism and the U.S. chemical industry. Acad Manag J 42(4):351–371
Hofstede G (1981) Management control of public and not-for-profit activities. Acc Organ Soc 6 (3):193–211
Hopper T, Powel A (1985) Making Sense of research into the organizational and social aspects of management accounting: a review of its underlying assumptions. J Manage Stud 22(5): 429–465
Hopper T, Otley D, Scapens B (2001) British Management accounting research: whence and whither: opinions and recollections. Brit Acc Rev 33(3):263–291
Hopwood AG (1987) The archeology of accounting systems. Acc Organ Soc 12(3):207–234
Hopwood AG (1988) Accounting from the outside: the collected papers of Anthony G Hopwood. Garland. Hopwood, AG, New York and London
Hoque M, Ji Z, Zheng D, Luo W, Li W, You B, Park JY, Yehia G, Tian B (2013) Analysis of alternative cleavage and polyadenylation by 39 region extraction and deep sequencing. Nat Methods 10:133–139
Howard-Grenville JA (2005) The persistence of flexible organizational routines: the role of agency and organizational context. Organ Sci 16(6):618–636
Huang HC (2009) Designing a knowledge-based system for strategic planning: a balanced scorecard perspective. Expert Syst Appl 36(1):209–218
Hussain MM, Hoque Z (2002) Understanding non-financial performance measurement practices in Japanese banks: a new institutional sociology perspective. Acc Auditing Accountability J 15 (2):162–183
Innes J, Norris G (1997) The use of activity-based information—A managerial perspective. CIMA, London

Innes J, Mitchell F (1990a) The process of change in management accounting: some field study evidence. Manag Acc Res 1(1):3–19
Innes J, Mitchell F (1990b). Activity-based costing: a review with case studies. CIMA, London
Innes J, Mitchell F (1995) A survey of activity-based costing in the UK's largest companies. Manag Acc Res 6(2):137–153
Jensen JC, Berg N (2012) Determinants of traditional sustainability reporting versus integrated reporting. An institutionalist approach. Bus Strategy Environ 21(5):299–316
Johnson D (1998) Identification and selection of environmental performance indicators: application of the balanced scorecard approach. Corp Environ Strategy 5(4):34–41
Johnson T, Kaplan RS (1987) The relevance lost: the rise and fall of management accounting. Harvard Business School Press, Boston
Jones O, Craven M (2001) Expanding capabilities in a mature manufacturing firm: absorptive capacity and the TCS. Int Small Bus J 19(3):39–55
Jones TC, Dugdale D (1998) Theory of constraints: transforming ideas? Brit Acc Rev 30(1):73–91
Kaplan RS (1986) Accounting lag—Obsolescence of cost accounting systems. Calif Manag Rev 28(2):174–199
Kanter RM, Stein BA, Jick TD (1992) The challenge of organisational change. The Free Press, New York, NY
Kaplan RS, Anderson SR (2004) Timedriven activity-based costing. Harvard Bus Rev 82 (11):131–138
Kaplan RS, Norton DP (1996) The balanced scorecard: translating strategy into action Boston. Harvard Business School Press, Boston
Kaplan RS, Norton DP (1992) The Balanced scorecard: measures that drive performance. Harvard Bus Rev 83(7):1–11
Kasurinen T (2002) Exploring Management accounting changes: the case of balanced scorecard implementation. Manag Acc Res 13(3):323–343
Kieffer T (2005) Feeling bad: antecedents and consequences of negative emotions in ongoing change. J Organ Behav 26(8):875–897
Kostova T, Roth K (2002) Adoption of an organisational practice by subsidiaries of multinational corporations: institutional and relational effects. Acad Manag J 45(1):215–233
Kotter JP (1995) Leading change: Why transformation efforts fail. Harvard Bus Rev 73(2):59–67
Kotter JP (1996) Leading change. Harvard Business School Press, Boston
Kotter JP, Cohen DS (2002) Creative ways to empower action to change the organization: cases in point. J Organ Excellence 22(1):73–82
Laitinen EK (2001) Management accounting change in small technology companies: towards a mathematical model of the technology firm. Manag Acc Res 12(4):507–541
Laitinen Erkki K (2006) Explaining management accounting change: evidence from finland international journal of accounting. Auditing Perform Eval 3(2):252–281
Lapsley I, Pettigrew A (1994) Meeting the challenge: accounting for change. Financ Accountability Manag 10(2):79–92
Lapsley I, Wright E (2004) The diffusion of management accounting innovations in the public sector: a research agenda. Manag Acc Res 15(3):355–374
Larrinaga C, Bebbington J (2001) Environmental accounting practices—Organisational change or institutional appropriation. Crit Perspect Acc 12(3):269–292
Laughlin RC (1991) Environmental disturbances and organizational transitions and transformations: some alternative models. Organ Stud 1(2):209–232
Laughlin R, Broadbent J, Willig-Atherton H (1994) Recent financial and administrative changes in GP practices in the UK: initial experiences and effects. Acc Auditing Accountability J 7(3): 96–124
Lawrence PR, Lorsch JW (1986) Organization and environment: managing differentiation and integration. Harvard Business School Classics
Lewin K (1946) Action research and minority problems. J Soc Issues 2(4):34–46
Lewin K (1947) Frontiers in group dynamics: concept, method and reality in social science; social equilibria and social change. Hum Relat

Lewin K (1951) Field theory in social science, selected theoretical papers, In: Cartwright D, Harpers D (ed) New York, NY
Libby T, Waterhouse JH (1996) Predicting change in management accounting systems. J Manag Acc Res 8:137–150
Lines R (2005) The structure and function of attitudes toward organizational change. Hum Resour Dev Rev 4(1):8–32
Lord BR (2007) Strategic management accounting. In: Hopper T, Northcott D, Scapens R (eds) Issues in management accounting. FT/Prentice Hall, Harlow
Lounsbury M, Crumley ET (2007) New practice creation: an institutional perspective on innovation. Organ Stud 28(7):993–1012
Luecke R (2003) Managing change and transition. Harvard Business Press, Bostan
Malmi T (1997) Towards explaining activity-based costing failure: accounting and control in a decentralized organization. Manag Acc Res 8(4):459–480
Malmi T (1999) Activity-based costing diffusion across organizations: an exploratory empirical analysis of Finnish firms. Acc Organ Soc 24(8):649–672
May M, Bryan T (1999) Value based management at British aerospace. Manag Acc 77:36–37
McKinley W, Mone MA (2003) Micro and macro perspectives in organization theory: a tale of incommensurability. The oxford handbook of organization theory. Oxford University Press, Oxford, pp 345–372
McLaren J (1999) A strategic perspective on economic value added. Manag Acc 77:30–32
Mecca TV (2004) Basic concepts of organizational change for administrative leaders. Pacific Crest, Lisle
Meyer JW, Rowan B (1991) Institutionalized organizations: Formal structure as myth and ceremony. In: Powell WW, DiMaggio PJ (eds) The new institutionalism in organizational analysis. University of Chicago Press, Chicago, pp 41–62
Meyer J, Scott WR (1992) Centralization and the legitimacy problems of local government. In: Meyer J, Scott WR (eds) Organizational environments: Ritual and rationality. Sage, Newbury Park
Meyer JW, Scott WR (eds) (1994) Institutional environments and organizations: Structural complexity and individualism. Sage, Tohusan
Meyer JW, Rowan B (1977) Institutionalized organizations: formal structure as myth and ceremony. Am J Sociol
Miller D, Friesen PH (1984) A longitudinal study of the corporate life cycle. Manage Sci 30: 1161–1183
Miller P (1991) Accounting innovation beyond the enterprise: problematizing investment decisions and programming economic growth in the UK in the 1960s. Acc Organ Soc 16 (8):733–762
Miller P, Power M (2013) Accounting, organizing, and economizing: Connecting accounting research and organization theory. Acad Manag Annals 7(1):557–605
Mintzberg H (1979) The structuring of organizations. Prentice-Hall, Englewood Cliffs
Mintzberg H (1981) Organization design: fashion or fit? Harvard Bus Rev 59
Modell S (2007) Management accounting change. In: Hopper T, Scapens RW et al (eds) Issues in management accounting. Financial Times Prentice Hall, Harlow
Moll J, Burns J, Major M (2006) Institutional theory. In: Moll J, Burns J, Major M, Hoque Z (eds) Methodological Issues in accounting research: theories, methods and issues. Spiramus, London, pp 183–205
Moores K, Yuen S (2001) Management accounting systems and organizational configuration: a life-cycle perspective. Acc Organ Soc 26(4):351–389
Mouritsen J (1994) Rationality, institutions and decision making; reflections on March and Olsen's rediscovering institutions. Acc Organ Soc 19(2):193–211
Napier CJ (2006) Accounts of change: 30 years of historical accounting research. Acc Organ Soc 31(4):445–507

Nelson RR (1994). 'Routines'. In: Hodgson G, Samuels W, Tool W (eds) The Elgar Companion to Istitutional and Evoluntary Economics, vol 2, pp 249–53. Edward Elgar, Aldershot and Brookfield

North D (1990) Institutions, institutional change and economic performance. Cambridge University Press, Cambridge

Oliver C (1991) Strategic responses to institutional processes. Acad Manag Rev 16(1):145–179

Oliver C (1992) The antecedents of deinstitutionalization. Organ Stud 13(4):563–588

Ostrom E (1999) Institutional rational choice. In: Sabatier PA (ed) Theories of the policy process. Westview Press, Boulder, pp 35–72

Padovani E, Orelli RL, Young DW (2014) Implementing change in a hospital management accounting system. Public Manag Rev 16(8):1184–1204

Palmer D, Biggart NW (2002) Organizational institutions. In: Baum JAC (ed) Companion of organization. Blakwall, Oxford, pp 259–280

Parto S (2005) Economic activity and institutions: taking stock. J Econ Issues 39(1):21–53

Pearce JL (2001) Organization and management in the embrace of government. Erlbaum, Mahwah

Pentland B, Haerem T, Hillison D (2010) Comparing organisational routines as recurrent patterns of action. Organ Stud 31(7):917–940

Perera S, McKinnon JL, Harrison GL (2003) Diffusion of transfer pricing innovation in the context of commercialization—A longitudinal case study of a government trading enterprise. Manag Acc Res 14(2):140–164

Pettigrew AM, Whipp R (1993) Understanding the environment. In: Mabey C, MayonWhite B (eds) Managing change, 2nd edn. The Open University/Paul Chapman Publishing, London

Pettigrew AM, Ferlie EF, McKee L (1992) Shaping strategic change. Sage, London

Pfeffer J (1992) Managing with power: politics and influence in organizations. Harvard Business School Press, Boston

Pfeffer J, Salancik GR (1978) The external control of organizations: a resource dependence perspective. Harper and Row, New York

Quattrone P, Hopper T (2001) What does organizational change mean? Speculations on a taken for granted category. Manag Acc Res 12(4):403–435

Quinn RE (2010) Deep change: Discovering the leader within. Wiley, San Francisco

Ribeiro JA, Scapens RW (2006) Institutional theories in management accounting change: contributions, issues and paths for development. Qual Res Acc Manag 3(2):94–111

Robertson PJ, Seneviratne SJ (1995) Outcomes of planned organizational change in the public sector: a meta-analytic comparison to the private sector. Public Adm Rev 55(6):547–558

Rowbottom N, Locke J (2016) The emergence of <IR>. Accounting and Business Research, 46(1):83–115

Ryan B, Scapens RW, Theobold M (2002) Research method and methodology in finance and accounting. Thomson Learning, London

Scapens RW (1990) Researching management accounting practice: the role of case study research methods. Brit Acc Rev 22(3):259–281

Scapens RW (1994) Never mind the gap: towards an institutional perspective on management accounting practice. Manag Acc Res 5(3):301–321

Scapens RW (1999) Broadening the scope of management accounting: from a micro-economic to a broader business perspective. Unknown Journal

Scapens RW (2006) Understanding management accounting practices: a personal journey. Brit Acc Rev 38(1):1–30

Scapens RW, Roberts J (1993) Accounting and control: a case study of resistance to accounting change. Manag Acc Res 4(1):1–32

Schalk R, Campbell JW, Freese C (1998) Change and employee behaviour. Leadersh Organ Dev J 19(3):157–163

Scott WR (1991) The politics of deviance: stigma contests and the use of power. Prentice-Hall, Englewood Cliffs

Scott WR (1998) Organizations: rational, natural, and open systems (4th ed). Prentice Hall and Upper Saddle River

Scott WR (2001a) Institutions and organizations (2ed). Sage, Thousand Oaks
Scott WR (2001b) Organizations, overview. International Encyclopedia of the Social and Behavioral Sciences, Pergamon/Elsevier Science, Amsterdam
Scott WR (2003) Organizations. Relational, natural, and open systems. Pearson. Upper Saddle River, New Jersey
Scott WR, Meyer JW (1983) The organization of societal sectors. In: John WM, Richard Scott W (eds) Organizational environments: ritual and rationality. Sage, Beverly Hills, pp 129–153
Shank JK (1996) Analysing technology investments-from NPV to strategic cost management. Manag Acc Res 7(2):185–197
Sharman PA (2003) The case for management accounting. Strategic Financ
Shaw P (1997) Intervening in the shadow systems of organizations: Consulting from a complexity perspective. J Organ Change 10(3):235–250
Shields M, Young SM (1991) Managing product life cycle cost: an organizational model. J Cost Manag 15–22
Shields MD (1995) An empirical analysis of firms' implementation experiences with activity-based costing. J Manag Acc Res 7(1):148–165
Soin K, Seal W, Cullen J (2002) ABC and Organizational change: an institutional perspective. Manag Acc Res 13(2):249–271
Spraakman G (2006) The impact of institutions on management accounting changes at the Hudson's Bay Company, 1670 to 2005. J Acc Organ Change 2(2):101–122
Stensaker B (2004) The transformation of organisational identities: interpretations of policies the concerning the quality of teaching and learning in Norwegian higher education. University of Twente
Stubbs W, Higgins C (2014) Integrated REPORTING AND INTERNAL MECHANISMS OF CHANGE. Acc Auditing Acc J 27(7):1068–1089
Sulaiman S, Mitchell F (2005) Utilising a typology of management accounting change: an empirical analysis. Manag Acc Res 16(4):422–437
Tomkins C (2001) Interdependencies, trust and information in relationships, alliances and networks. Acc Organ Soc 26(2):161–191
Vaivio J (1999) Exploring a non-financial management accounting change. Manag Acc Res 10 (4):409–437
Van de Ven AH, Poole MS (1995) Explaining development and change in organizations. Acad Manag Rev 510–540
Vatn A (2005) Institutions and the environment. Edward Elgar, Cheltenham
Waldron M (2005) Overcoming barriers to change in management accounting systems. J Am Acad Bus 6(2):244–249
Wallander J (1999) Budgeting-an unnecessary evil. Scand J Manag 15(4):405–421
Wanderley DAC, Cullen J, Tsamenyi M (2011) Privatisation and electricity sector reforms in Brazil: accounting perspective. J Acc Emerg Econ 1(1):53–75
Weber PS, Weber JE (2001) Changes in employee perceptions during organizational change. Leadersh Organ Dev J 22(6):291–300
Wickramasinghe D, Alawattege C (2007) Management accounting change: approaches and perspectives. Routledge, London/New York
Wicks D (2001) Institutionalized mindsets of invulnerability: Differentiated institutional fields and the antecedents of organizational crisis. Organ Stud 22(4):659–692
Wild S, Van Staden CJ (2013). Integrated reporting: initial analysis of early reporters—An institutional theory approach. 7th Asia Pacific interdisciplinary accounting research conference, Kobe, pp 1–39
Williamson OE (1985) The economic institutions of capitalism. Free Press, New York
Williams JJ, Seaman AE (2001) Predicting change in management accounting systems: national culture and industry effects. Acc Organ Soc 26(4):443–460
Williamson OE (2000) The new institutional economics: taking stock, looking ahead. J Econ Lit 38(3):595–613
Wilson DC (1992) A strategy of change. Routledge, London

Yazdifar H (2003) Management accounting in the twenty-first-century firm: a strategic view. Strategic Change 12(2):109–113

Yoshikawa T, Innes J, Mitchell F (1995) A Japanese case study of functional cost analysis. Manag Acc Res 6(4):415–432

Zucker L (1983) Organizations as institutions. In: Bacharach SB (ed) Research in sociology of organizations. Jai Press, Greenwich

Chapter 3
Principles, Concepts and Elements of Integrated Reporting

Abstract The chapter guides the reader in a tour along the development of Integrated Reporting. Most of the emerging literature on Integrated Reporting has identified the sustainability report as being the necessary antecedent. However, a deep understanding of Integrated Reporting requires one to consider similarities and differences with other documents produced annually by an organization. The chapter provides an overview of different accountability tools generally adopted for accountability purposes (annual report, corporate governance report, corporate social responsibility report and intellectual capital report), driving the reader to a panoramic view of the two different frameworks on integrated reporting developed so far: the South Africa Integrated Reporting Framework and the International <IR> Framework. Some reflections on the challenges of Integrated Reporting conclude the chapter, leading the reader to the last chapter, where a case study analyzing the ongoing management accounting change process toward the adoption of the Integrated Reporting in a public organization is discussed.

Keywords Integrated reporting · Annual report · Corporate governance report · Corporate social responsibility report · Intellectual capital report · Frameworks

3.1 The Integrated Reporting Movement

Integrated Reporting could be seen as the latest development in a long line of proposed innovations in the domain of alternative forms of corporate reporting. In 1992, the United Nations Conference on Environment and Development (UNCED) stated the concept of sustainable development as a public policy goal, calling for non-State actors to participate. Since then, a large number of corporate social responsibility (CSR), sustainability and environmental, social and governance (ESG) standards and guidelines have been issued worldwide by national and

This chapter was written by Francesca Manes Rossi.

E. Katsikas et al., *Towards Integrated Reporting*,
SpringerBriefs in Accounting, DOI 10.1007/978-3-319-47235-5_3

international standard setters and organizations, both for public and private entities (an overview in Bendell et al. 2011).

Integrated reporting has been generally considered as the answer to the need of attaining a more holistic approach of corporate activity, embedding in a unique report the fundamental contents of other forms of corporate reporting. The idea is to overcome the view of separate reports (e.g. sustainability, governance, environmental, etc.) supporting financial reporting, and to look for a tool in which all the information cannot be simply added to each other but rather integrated into "One Report" (Eccles and Krzus 2010a).

However, the process of definition of the principles, contents and elements to be considered while preparing an Integrated Reporting has been nothing but simple and clear.

As observed by the GRI in a survey published in 2013, "no globally accepted standards or practices exist with regard to what an integrated report should cover and how it should be constructed to meet the needs of its users. Neither is there clarity on who exactly integrated reports' users are, or how such reports should ultimately be appraised for quality and substance" (GRI 2013: 7).

There has been a step forward with the issue of the international <IR> framework in December 2013 by the International Integrated Reporting Council (IIRC). The IIRC has signed memorandums of understanding with other institutions including organizations by which it was constituted, as with Accounting for Sustainability Project (A4S), the Global Reporting Initiative (GRI) and the International Federation of Accountants (IFAC), and also the Carbon Disclosure Project (CDP), the Climate Disclosure Standards Board (CDSB) and the World Intellectual Capital Initiative (WICI) (http://www.ifrs.org/Alerts/PressRelease/Pages/IASB-and-IIRC-sign-MoU.aspx).

In this chapter, principles, concepts and elements of Integrated Reporting are tackled. First, the evolution that led to the establishment of the Integrated Reporting is discussed. Then a comparison among the annual report, corporate governance report, corporate social responsibility report, intellectual capital report and integrated report is presented, with the aim of focusing on what is "new" in the Integrated Report. The fourth paragraph offers a summary of the frameworks and guidelines dealing with the Integrated Reporting. The fifth paragraph focalizes on the movement towards the adoption of IR undertaken in practice. Challenges of the Integrated Reporting are discussed in the last paragraph.

3.2 From Sustainability Reports to Integrated Reports

Social and environmental reporting have a long tradition, both in the private and in public sector (Guthrie and Parker 1989; Gray 2001; Adams 2004), as a result of the criticism towards the ability of financial reporting in communicating the whole performance of the organizations. Some scholars have considered the incapacity of the financial report to fully disclose intangible assets, and this represents a failure in responding to the original information function of financial reporting (Amir and Lev 1996).

Several attempts to regulate and standardize these wide sets of corporate reporting have been undertaken. Over time, among others, reporting guidelines and standards have been developed by the GRI, A4S, WICI, the Enhanced Business Reporting Consortium (EBRC), CDP, the International Corporate Governance Network (ICGN), the Sustainability Accounting Standards Board (SASB) and CDSB. As noted by scholars, overlaps and duplications occur among the different documents prepared (Bendell et al. 2011) and the differences in the kind of reports concretely adopted by organization are extremely wide (Guthrie and Farneti 2008).

Scholars have discussed at length how to interpret the flourishing of these types of reports and most of them considered social and environmental reporting as accountability tools (Gray et al. 1988; Bebbington et al. 2014), while others have examined this trend in an effort to gain legitimacy (Deegan et al. 2002). However, some criticism has been raised against the idea that the pursuit of corporate legitimacy can be considered as the primary rational for disclosure (Guthrie and Parker 1989). In this vein the idea that the adoption of Integrated Reporting is the result of a management accounting change has been embraced, and disclosure is seen as the final step that flourishes from the progressive (and ongoing) institutionalization process inside the organization of integrated thinking (Higgins et al. 2014).

The evolution of the concept, application and development of Integrated Reporting has been examined by Eccles et al. (2015) and four main phases have been recognized (Fig. 3.1).

a. *Company experimentation*: since the early 2000s, some companies start to produce such a report, combining financial and non-financial data in a meaningful way.

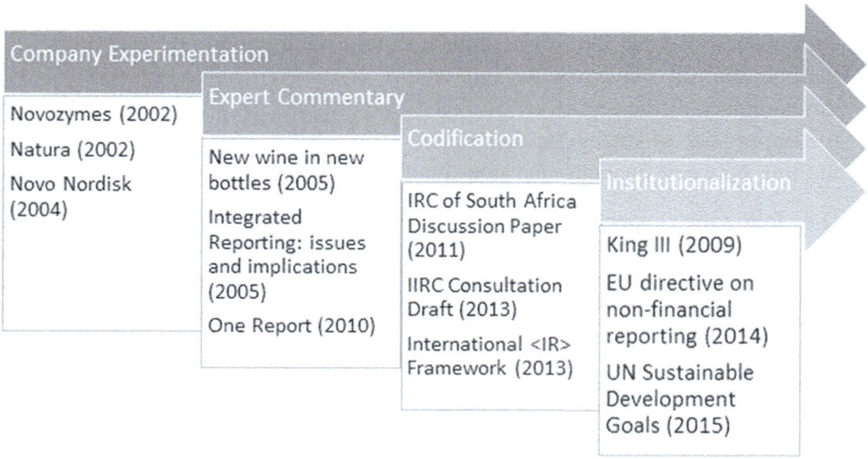

Fig. 3.1 The four phases of the evolution of the integrated report (Eccles et al. 2015: 32)

b. *Expert Commentary*: consultants, academics, experts and think tanks start to reflect on the first experiences published by pioneers and two publications appear in the 2005.
c. *Codification*: the need for a common framework, principles and rules emerges and several standards and guidelines are prepared.
d. *Institutionalization*: since King III in South Africa is approved, there is an increasing movement to influence regulators and organizations towards the adoption of the Integrated Reporting.

The aforementioned phases are reported hereafter, summarizing Eccles et al. (2015) views, to give a better understanding of the Integrated Reporting evolution and shed light on the current practices.

Company experimentation

Similarly, to many other management ideas resulting from an accounting change process, the birthplace of integrated reporting can be identified in practice. The proof lies in the fact that the three forerunners, namely Novozymes, Novo Nordisk and Natura, all began independently in the same year of 2002. All of them considered the need to communicate sustainability issues as being essential to the long-term success of their companies. Thus, in these first experiences the information function was fundamental. The idea behind the adoption of this new tool was to provide "one report" that would be able to demonstrate the existing link between sustainable management and corporate performance. Of course these first experiences present differences in their execution, because at those times the guidelines provided by the GRI on sustainability had just been issued; moreover, the understanding of what it means was limited in this phase. However, some fundamental issues identified by the three companies involved in the experimental phase continued to be newsworthy, such as:

- the need for materiality and stakeholder engagement;
- the question of what kind of assurance should be provided on the report;
- the possible role played by the internet;
- the boundary of the report;
- the importance of intangible assets;
- the link between financial and non-financial performance measures.

The following experience, in 2008, by Philips and United Technologies Corporation added further noteworthy elements. While the former described the process bringing the issue to the document, and the latter raised the concern about concision and the possibility to reduce, all in all, information provided to stakeholders.

Expert Commentary

This phase is characterized by the efforts played by consultants, academics, experts and think tanks to reflect on the first experiences published by pioneers. Following the first experience of Integrated Reporting, two publications appear within a few months of each other in 2005:

- *New Wine in New Bottles*: written by Allen White, Vice President and Senior Fellow of Tellus Institute, a non-profit research and policy organization. While focusing on non-financial reporting, White mentioned "integrated reporting" referring to the experiences examined as the "next generation reporting" (White 2005).
- *The Solstice/Vancity Study*: this study on integrated reporting, published by a Canadian sustainability consulting firm called Solstice (Solstice Sustainability Works, 2005) together with Vancity Bank, consider Integrated Reporting as the combination of financial and sustainability reporting, demanding for a stronger integration. The fundamental question raised by the study was "Does integrated reporting encourage holistic management or does a holistic management approach naturally lead to integrated reporting?" (p. 7).

In 2010 Eccles and Krzus published "One report", the first book entirely dedicated to Integrated Reporting. This is also the period in which academics started to observe and study this new tool, discussing the content, the process and the organizational changes connected with the preparation of the new report, as well as the internalization of the "integrated thinking" concept (Jensen and Berg 2012). In this first book the responsibilities of all key actors in making integrated reporting a common practice are discussed. Moreover, consultant companies started to promote the idea of integration in company reports, and studies and publications on the matter started to appear (KPMG 2010; PwC South Africa 2010).

Codification

While the first two phases are characterized by the efforts of single organizations or experts, in the third phase, there emerged a common effort by an authoritative body, in defining the concept of integrated reporting and related principles and guidelines, to support the implementation of this tool. A multi-stakeholders approach seems to stem from these first definition attempts and the transformation functions (Eccles and Serafeim 2014) of integrated reporting emerged.

Two most relevant bodies led them during this period, albeit with a different degree of authoritative power and legitimacy, The Integrated Reporting Committee of South Africa and the International Integrated Reporting Council.

The former is a body generated by the government with the specific duty of preparing a framework for Integrated Reporting, while the second one is a non-governmental organization with no legal power to issue mandate regulations, but with a high consensus and large support by other standard setters and international organizations. While the structure and fundamental concepts belonging to the documents issued by the two bodies will be discussed in the fourth paragraph, it is worth underlining the extent to which the concept of value creation emerged, as well as the need to represent the cooperation of all the "capitals" throughout the value creation process.

Institutionalization

The last phase, still undergoing, has been defined by Eccles et al. (2015) as "Institutionalization" because of King III in South Africa. Currently it can be identified by a strong attempt to influence regulators and the market towards the adoption and a concrete use of Integrated Reporting, with a number of progressively increasing mandatory requirements. Even if the IIRC does not have any regulatory power, it has a quite ambitious approach of being considered as a worldwide benchmark for the preparation of the Integrated Reporting.

However, it should be noted that in the institutionalization phase some criticisms start to emerge in the literature which deserve full consideration, which is discussed in the last paragraph.

3.3 Different Reports for Different Purposes: The Need for IR

As stated above, integrated reporting was born through the experience of some pioneer organizations answering the need for overcoming the publication of several reports beside the annual financial report. In fact, at the beginning social and environmental disclosure were both included in the financial report but, in the past two decades, the number of stand-alone reports, coupled with other communication tools—like websites—has dramatically increased. Moreover, a recent research conducted by E&Y (2015a) highlights the growing attention payed by investors to non-financial information: according to the published results, the percentage of respondents who consider mandatory board oversight of non-financial performance reporting to be "essential" or "important" equals 80 % (in comparison with 36 % in 2014).

For this reason, it worth paying attention to the evolution and limitations of at least four kinds of reports, namely the *annual report*, the *corporate governance report*, the *corporate social responsibility report*, and the *intellectual capital report*, in respect to the possible added value of the *integrated report*. An integrated report constitutes, in some way, the evolution of corporate reporting over the last decades, representing the cutting-edge in the field. To this aim, the following analysis is targeted to progressively emphasize different factors that have led to the development of the IR.

3.3.1 Annual Report

The annual report has been analysed by scholars for a long time. They focused their attention mainly on the content of financial reporting, whilst the theoretical development about the role of corporate reporting is relatively recent. Main areas of interests concerned the discussion of the decision-making (Vergoossen 1993;

Bouwman et al. 1987), the stewardship (e.g. O'Connell 2007; Abdel-Khalik 2011) and the informative function of the document (Watts 1977; Jensen and Meckling 1976). Standard setters have specially emphasised the decision-making function (see IASB Conceptual Framework 2010), even if considerable attention has been also paid to the accountability function in the public domain (IPSASB Conceptual Framework 2014).

In the last years there has been a growing attention to the informativeness of disclosure, especially focusing on its attitude to provide a complete picture of strategies and plans, allowing the inclusion of a forward-looking view to the backward traditional view (Lang and Lundholm 1996). Several researches have demonstrated that a better disclosure supports firms in obtaining financial resources in more favourable terms (e.g. Botosan 1997).

It worth noting that some scholars, in regard to public sector entities, criticize the possible overload of information, which can turn into a flood of misinformation (Grimmelikhuijsen et al. 2013). A state of disclosure overloaded was perceived also in relation to private sector entities (ACCA 2012a) and several initiatives have been undertaken to eliminate the redundant material in the Corporate Annual Report (e.g. FASB project on Disclosure 2015; EFRAG et al. 2012). The need to reduce the level of growing complexity in the disclosure was underlined also by scholars, both in terms of financial information and accounting measures adopted, as well as non-financial information embedded in the disclosure (Leung et al. 2015).

As already noted, a further limitation of the annual report is the lack of in depth information relating to some issues that can be relevant for stakeholders, such as management quality, customer satisfaction, environmental and social performance (Fasan 2013).

In addition, despite several efforts undertaken to include some forward looking information in the financial reporting, the annual report does not offer a clear explanation of the value creation process nor does it support the prediction of the long-term performance of the entity. This would also affect the performance of management. Having a short- rather than a long-term view in the decision-making process would negatively affect the way in which a company is managed, possibly determining a lower attention to the research and development issue, as well as the growth of the employees and also to customer loyalty.

Table 3.1 shows the main features of the annual report compared with the other reports. In this comparison, it is of value to highlight that being based on a strong set of accounting principles; the annual report generally presents a higher comparability as well as a higher level of assurance, in comparison with other reporting documents.

3.3.2 Corporate Governance Report

The Corporate Governance Report is usually devoted to illustrate the governance structure characterizing the company. In accordance with the specific regulation in place in different countries, it explains how the entity is organized, including the role played by different committees responsible for specific tasks, such as setting strategy, internal audit, or remuneration strategies. The first example of regulation about this report is quite recent, (Cadbury's Report 1992), and is basically focused in clarifying the responsibility of board of directors and the auditors committee, as well as the distribution of roles amongst different boards and committees within the company.

Corporate governance practices are contingent on the institutional environment being generally related to the code of company governance (Aguilera 2005). However, the different regulations generally deal with the balance between individual and communal goals, as well as economic and social goals.

The publication of an annual report is generally mandatory in most of the economic developed countries: following the example of the United States' Sarbanes-Oxley Act, rules relating to corporate governance mechanism have been issued in approximately 90 nations (Haxhi and Aguilera 2015). Moreover, supranational organizations (like EU and OECD) have provided corporate governance guidelines, basically addressed to regulated and standardized corporate governance mechanisms, and consequently the content of the report. The approach followed has been mostly devoted to protect shareholders (i.e. minorities) and to assure suppliers of financial resources (Kolk 2008).

Thus, while this reports adds information on the role played by different bodies operating inside the company, as well as explaining the role covered by executive and non-executive directors and clarifying their responsibility and their behaviour during the year, it does not discuss any relation with the performance of the company, therefore enclosed information is totally separated by those incorporated in the annual reports. In this regard, the need for an integrated approach which is able to clarify the connection between the roles played by managers, directors and members of other boards, strategic choices and the value-creation process, are the areas of information which are strongly desirable and required by different categories of stakeholders. In fact, the behaviour of managers, directors and members of the other boards would affect the future of the company and the related performance.

3.3.3 Reporting About Sustainability and Environmental Issue

While annual reports and corporate governance reports are mandatory in most of OECD countries, Sustainability Reports (SR), Corporate Social Responsibility Reports (CSR), Environmental, Social and Governance Reports (ESG) and Carbon Disclosure Reports (CD) are almost voluntary. The first two terms are often used as synonyms even if each one dedicates a strong attention to specific aspects, and even if different standards have been prepared to support their preparation and diffusion.

A trend in asking for more non-financial information is undeniable in the last decades, as the large production of guidelines, recommendations and standards provided worldwide demonstrates. Among the other, two bodies in particular have played a leading role: the Global Reporting Initiatives (GRI) and the Accounting for Sustainability (A4S). Both assume that this kind of report should give an account on their social and environmental impacts.

The *GRI* started in 2000 by issuing the first set of guidelines. However several criticism have arisen: the GRI has been blamed due to the lack of investors involvement (Cooper and Morgan 2013), and because the report presents a low comparability (Van Wensen et al. 2011). The GRI version 3.1 (issued in 2011) intends to capture through performance indicators six different dimensions: economic, environmental, labour practices and decent work, human rights, society, and product responsibility. A further version, issued in 2013 (G4), has been prepared after a consultation, trying to improve harmonization with other reporting standards. Moreover, the GRI has launched a new project, Sustainability and Reporting 2025, aimed at addressing the new challenges and developments in corporate reporting (GRI 2016).

Since its creation in 2004 the *A4S* moved towards the so-called "Connected Reporting" in the aim of integrating financial, narrative and sustainability information (Druckman and Fries 2010). This is the first attempt to conceptualize the importance of focussing not only on the reporting as an output of the process, but also on the process of reporting itself. Moreover, the investors are considered to be the main audience of the document.

A further step towards a more integrated view of environmental and sustainability information has been completed by the *UN Global Compact* (UN Global Compact 2014). The main aim was to align organisations' strategies and operations with a set of ten accepted principles, covering four different areas (human rights, labour, environment and anti-corruption) to be integrated into the organization strategies and operations. Basically, the UN Global Compact promotes a different managerial approach to corporate sustainability, rather than a specific model of reporting. In this sense, it makes reference to other standards prepared by different organizations (UN Global Compact 2014).

Among the different reports, an opposite attention should be also dedicated to the *Carbon Disclosure Project* (CDP), specially focused on carbon footprint disclosure. This represents a form of market self-regulation, intended to overcome the limitation of Kyoto protocol, aimed at encouraging companies adopting and disclosing policies that address these specific issue.

All in all, it can be affirmed that professional investors and financial analysts require more information on these matters (Solomon and Solomon 2006; Eccles et al. 2015) with the aim of better supporting the assessment of the future performance. In the same vein, public entities have the responsibility to manage public resources in the interest of the community and, as noted by the GRI (2005), are expected to publicly and transparently report their efforts in promoting sustainability. A growing body of research has been developed on this issue, even exploring experiences in different kinds of public sector entities (Guthrie and Farneti 2008; Farneti and Guthrie 2009; Ball et al. 2014).

Moreover, it worth noting that the European Union (EU), with a recent regulation (Directive 2014/95/EU, which amends the previous one 2013/34/EU) have further encouraged large companies (like listed companies, insurance, or companies with more than 500 employees) to provide a better disclosure of social and environmental information, including in the management report a non-financial statement specifically dedicated to the abovementioned issues. Additionally, a public consultation has been recently undertaken by the EU (closed on 15th April 2016) to recognise the point of view of different stakeholders about a set of non-binding guidelines to support the development of this information. The direction undertaken by the EU seems to move towards an integrated report, considering that the different areas (environmental, employee and social issues, human rights and anti-corruption) should also take into consideration the underlining business model and policies related to the previous matter.

Exploring the differences between the several kinds of CSR reports and IR is enormously important for managers, as it helps to acquire the proper consciousness on conditions needed to implement this new tool, as well as on the relevant necessary knowledge for its preparation (Fasan 2013).

In this regard, from an institutional perspective, the role played by the economic, social and legal context in the diffusion of IR deserves investigation. As previous research reveals, there is a non-significant incidence of the legal systems dominating in a certain country (civil vs. common law) on the choice between traditional sustainability reports and IR (Jensen and Berg 2012), even if civil law countries are more inclined towards IR (Frías-Aceituno et al. 2013). Moreover, countries with a stronger investor protection and lower employment protection are more likely to adopt IR (Jensen and Berg 2012). In further analysis it would be useful to investigate if and how these relations are going to change, particularly throughout Europe. To this end, it must be noted that no research has been specifically devoted to public sector entities and few experiences have been reported at the moment in the IR database. However, in the aim of promoting new experiences, Ernest & Young (EY) has created the Excellence in Integrated Reporting Award for South African companies, including State-Owned Enterprises. Thus, in organizations belonging to the public sector, showing a motivation towards the adoption of IR deserves to be investigate through case studies.

3.3.4 Intellectual Capital Reporting

The concept of intellectual capital has been seen as being pivotal in the knowledge economy, and considered crucial in the creation of value in any kind of organization, as already discussed in the first chapter. Consequently, the need for new metrics, able to record and report the value attributable to IC, has emerged (Guthrie 2001). In the last two decades, literature dealing with the definition, the role, and the reporting of IC has grown tremendously (Ferenhof et al. 2015). Even in the public sector domain, especially in Universities, there has been a strong interest in emphasising the role of IC from several perspectives (Dumay et al. 2015; Massaro et al. 2015). Regulators and professional accounting bodies have encouraged companies to include IC disclosure in order to clarify the value creation process. Several initiatives have contributed to the promotion of IC disclosure (Abhayawansa 2014), the first one appearing in 1989 by the Kondrad Group to the consultation Draft of the WICI (*World Intellectual Capital Initiative*) Intangibles Reporting Framework, (for which the public consultation has just been closed in May 2016). All these initiatives and guidelines have progressively attempted to clarify what IC is, how it can be recognized, measured and disclosed offering some models as point of reference. According to Abhayawansa (2014), a first group of models basically deal with IC management, aiming at explaining value creation, while the others attempt to identify the knowledge gap or what is needed by the company to achieve its objectives. However, it must be said that none of these initiatives have assumed a leading role, leaving space for further interpretation and approaches. Consequently, a specific reporting model of IC has not been affirmed thus far. As reported by Eccles and Serafeim (2014), companies tend to provide greater information about financial capital and the use of natural resources rather than about the three typical components of IC (human, structural and relational capital). It worth noting that the last initiative, the one undertaken by WICI, is obtaining growing attention and the consultation process of the Consultation Draft of the Framework has contributed in attracting attention towards the proposed model. The WICI had already proposed a taxonomy which is codified under XBRL, including Key Value Driver that can be disclosed through a set of KPIs.

A growing attention to IC has also been paid by international accounting standards bodies which have required companies not only to describe IC resources in their reports, but to unravel the competitive advantages that investing and managing these resources can give. The American Institute of Certified Public Accountants (AICPA) formed in 1991 the well-known Jenkins Committee, which concluded its work by recommending a set of non-financial information that companies should provide in an external report. Later, in 1999, the Financial Accounting Standard Board (FASB), following the Jenkins Committee's work, set up several projects aimed at highlighting the importance of recognizing internally generated assets in financial statements, and of a systematic production of non-financial performance metrics, together with forward-looking information.

The OECD, since the mid-1990, has also promoted an agenda on measuring and reporting IC, while in 1998 the European Union launched the "Measuring Intangibles to Understand and improve innovation", which has produced a set of guidelines (MERITUM 2002). More recently, the IASB has furtherly promoted the development of information on IC with the Management Commentary Practice Statement in 2010.

According with Beattie and Smith, "listed companies face a mixture of mandatory and best practice guidance at national and supra-national level in relation to reporting on the intertwined concepts of intellectual capital and the business model" (2013: 244). Thus, the basic components for IC, and the way in which they are managed and measured, can be more correctly embedded in a report keen to discuss the business model adopted.

3.3.5 The Need for IR

The previous discussion has emphasized the relationship between the main features of different kinds of corporate reports and the features of IR. The Table 3.1 aims to offer a summary of the discussion undertaken.

It can be clearly observed that "Integrated reporting brings governance, financial capital, intellectual capital, social capital, and environmental capital onto a common platform" (Abeysekera 2013: 232).

It remains to unravel the dilemma if Integrated Reporting represents merely the evolution of the annual report or, on the contrary, if it is a form of the sustainability report. As highlighted by Fasan (2013), indubitably the integrated report could represent the best way to overcome some limitation of the annual report. It should be easier to understand, offer a long-term view, in addition to the view based on past results and the immediate future, and address non-financial information to give a better understanding of the overall performance of the organization. Simultaneously, it should match financial and non-financial data, embedding corporate governance issues, in a clearer approach than in traditional sustainability reports.

It is possible to conclude, according with Rowbottom and Locke (2016: 107) that "the IIRC emerged out of the co-incidence of pressures for a response to the financial crisis and the vacuum left by the failure of any of the many competing projects in the CSR/sustainability/ESG domain to achieve clear dominance".

The IIRC has been successful in attracting a wider recognition and support by influential institutions and actors, and has been noticed globally. However, the adoption of the framework can be done only on a voluntary basis. Some lessons could be learned in the following years reflecting on the experiences of South Africa. Nonetheless, difficulties in integrating what use to be separate pieces of corporate disclosure have to be taken into account (Abeysekera 2013).

Table 3.1 Comparing the features of different corporate reports

	Annual reports	CG report	CSR reports	IC report	Integrated report
Fundamental target	Specific stakeholders (shareholders and investors)	Specific stakeholders (shareholders and investors)	Several stakeholders (social and environmental perspective)	Several stakeholders	Primarily providers of financial capital but also other stakeholders
Mandatory versus voluntary	Mandatory	Mandatory	Voluntary (with few exceptions)	Voluntary (with few exception)	Voluntary (with one exceptions: South Africa)
Regulation or guidelines	National and international laws and accounting standards (GAAP or IAS/IFRS)	National and international codes	GRI Global reporting initiative or other national or international guidelines (A4S, OECD)	Several guidelines worldwide	IIRC framework
Content	Performance and overview of the firm	Organization's overview and governance	Potentially all contents elements related to social and environmental perspective	Intellectual capital	Potentially all contents elements related to the six capital
Comparability	High	Medium	Medium	Low	Low
Time orientation	Past and present (few information on the future)	Past and present	Past, present and future	Past, present and future	Past, present and future
Assurance level	High	High	Low	Low	Low

3.4 General Features, Frameworks and Guidelines for the Integrated Reporting

As discussed in the previous paragraph, IR gives an answer to the need of understanding the extent to which corporate social responsibility, intellectual capital and environmental strategies are linked in a specific entity and take part in the value creation process. Academics (e.g. Busco et al. 2013; Eccles and Krzus 2010b, Eccles et al. 2015; Mammatt 2009; Robertson and Samy 2015), audit firms (e.g. EY 2015a; PwC 2015; KPMG 2013, 2015), governments, interested groups and a large number of companies worldwide (see IIRC database) promote the adoption of one report including current and future perspectives of the company, encompassing both financial and non-financial measures and able to disclose strategies on value creation. Since 2013, the GRI database collected 1730 reports over several years, among which 46 were published by public agencies. The presence of IR issued by public entities demonstrates the interest in IR in the public domain, as already highlighted by scholars (Bartocci and Picciaia 2013).

As seen before, it has been claimed that IR overcomes some of the limitations of the Annual Report as well as traditional sustainability disclosure. For an in depth understanding of the IR tool, however, an examination of the principles and content of IR, proposed by the two principal frameworks available is required.

3.4.1 The South Africa Integrated Reporting Framework

South Africa represents an interesting case study because to date it is the only country in the world to mandate listed companies to provide integrated reporting on an "apply or explain" basis. The King Code of Corporate Governance Principles, the so-called King III, formally introduced the term 'integrated reporting' on 1 September 2009 proposing under different names some basic concepts underpinning the triple bottom line. Several circumstances might have led to the development of pioneering practices in corporate governance in South Africa (Eccles et al. 2015; Rowbottom and Locke 2016), first and foremost the need to attract capital by foreign investors, gaining trust in a business environment generally considered unreliable after forty-two years of Apartheid (de Villiers et al. 2014).

The Government established the King committee in 1992 to a create different business practice and environment, attuned to international comparison. The first Code of Corporate Principles, King I, was published in 1994 to advocate for total transparency. Principles embedded in this first version comprise a composition of the board of directors, the role of nonexecutive directors and their remuneration, effective auditing practice and encourage companies to adopt a Code of Ethics.

While the King I was a principle-based document, the Johannesburg stock exchange (JSE) made the code mandatory for listing on a "comply or explain" basis.

In 2002 a new Code, King II, was released. It included sections devoted to risk management, the role of the board, sustainability, and suggested that a company should adopt an internal audit charter. Moreover, it emphasised the fundamental role of non-financial information and their financial consequences for an organization. Somehow, the notion of the "integrated sustainability report" started to emerge, linking good corporate governance to sustainability and financial performance.

However, Kings I and II already placed South Africa at the vanguard of international corporate governance, King himself noticed that strategy and corporate governance issues where still separated by sustainability issues. Moreover, as a new Company act was released in 2008, a third code was needed. The new King III, published in 2009 and applicable from March 2010 onward, follows an "apply or explain" approach for its 76 principles and develops the concept of integrated reporting not just as a disclosure practice but as the result of "integrated thinking". Differences between King II and King III have been summarised in the ACCA (the Association of Chartered Certified Accountants) report (2012b). Moreover, King III advocates for independent assurance (Eccles et al. 2015).

In May 2010, as results of the joint efforts of the Association for Savings and Investment South Africa (ASISA), Business Unity South Africa (BUSA), Institute of Directors in South Africa (IoDSA), Johannesburg Stock Exchange (JSE Ltd) and the South African Institute of Chartered Accountants (SAIA), the Integrated Reporting Council of South Africa (IRC of SA) was established, with the aim of creating guidelines supporting South African companies in the preparation of IR.

In 2011, the Discussion Paper of the "Framework for Integrated Reporting and the Integrated Report Discussion Paper" was published (IRC of SA 2011).

Three categories of principles were identified:

- the principles informing the report *scope* and *boundary*;
- the principles informing the *selection of the report content* (including relevance and materiality, faithful representation, completeness, free from errors);
- the principles informing the *quality* of the reported information (comparability and consistency, verifiability; timeliness and understandability or clarity).

Moreover, elements to be included in the reports have been provided, as reported in the Table 3.2.

In March 2014, the Integrated Reporting Committee (IRC) of South Africa endorsed the International Integrated Reporting Framework (Framework), reconnecting in this way the two sets of principles. In this regard, it is worth noting that the King III Practice Note on The Integrated Report, (released in June 2014 by The Institute of Directors in Southern Africa), clarifies that King III offers the "what" of integrated reporting with the Framework offering the "how".

In December 2014, the IRC of South Africa issued a helpful paper for those organisations starting out on their integrated reporting journey, based on the <IR> Integrated Reporting Framework.

Table 3.2 Elements to be included in the integrated report (IRC of SA DP, p. 7)

• A description of the *scope and boundary* of the integrated report.
• A concise *overview of the organisation and its activities*, a statement of its *business model* describing the manner in which it currently creates value, and an overview of its *governance structure*.
• A description of the *risks and opportunities* that are material to the organisation's current and anticipated activities. These risks and opportunities are identified based on a review of financial, social, environmental, economic and governance issues and trends, an assessment of the organisation's material impacts on financial, social, economic and environmental systems, and a review of its relationships with key stakeholders.
• A description of the *organisation's strategic objectives* demonstrating how these have been informed by the risks and opportunities, including sustainability issues. The report should give an indication of the organisational competencies required to realise the strategic objectives, and a succinct list of the KPIs and KRIs that will track performance against the strategic objectives and competency requirements. This should cover the short-, medium- and long-term periods.
• An account of the *organisation's performance* in terms of its strategic objectives, its material social, environmental, economic and financial impacts, its KPIs and KRIs.
• A statement of the *organisation's anticipated activities and future performance objectives*, informed by its assessment of recent performance and understanding of societal trends and stakeholder expectations.
• An overview of *how the organisation remunerates employees and senior executives*, including factors that could influence future remuneration.
• A brief analytical commentary that reflects the understanding of the *organisation's governing structure and executive team* regarding the nature of the organisation's current and anticipated performance in the context of the organisation's strategic objectives. The organisation should report how it can improve its positive material impacts and how it can eradicate or ameliorate its negative material impacts.
Lastly, as resulted from systematic review that the biggest audit companies undertaken progressively (e.g. Deloitte 2015b; E&Y 2015b; KPMG 2015; PwC 2014) most of the top firms in South Africa still had to improve on several aspects of integrated reporting. However, since the introduction of King III, there is a clear trend towards this objective.

3.4.2 The <IR> Integrated Reporting Framework

Nowadays, the most comprehensive framework for integrated reporting is the Framework drafted by the International Integrated Reporting Council.

According to Rowbottom and Locke (2016) "as a standard setter of a voluntary reporting framework, the IIRC is in a position to influence corporate reporting without traditional sources of State legitimation" (p. 84). Is of value to identify and understand the interests inscribed in the framework by examining its origin and its contents.

3.4.2.1 The Origins of the <IR> Integrated Reporting Framework

Initiated by an agreement between the Accounting for Sustainability Project (A4S) and the Global Reporting Initiative (GRI) in August 2010, due to the emerging concept of integrated reporting promoted by King III in South Africa, the original mission of the IIRC was "to create a globally accepted integrated reporting framework which brings together financial, environmental, social and governance information in a clear, concise, consistent and comparable format" (as reported in Busco et al. 2013: 6). At this stage, the main users of IR seem to be investors and stakeholders involved in understanding how the organization is performing.

A first attempt to define a framework was completed in September 2011, when the Discussion Paper titled "Towards Integrated Reporting—Communicating Value in the 21st Century" was presented and a consultation phase was opened. Since then, the so-called Pilot Programme began to support the preparation of a specific Framework. In July 2012, the Draft Outline of the Integrated Reporting Framework was issued, incorporating information that emerged during the consultation period, with the specific aim of obtaining a large consensus and keep the audience aware of the process of development of the framework. The Prototype IR Framework was then released in November 2012, again as an interim step to discuss key concepts and principles representing the roots of Integrated Reporting. A number of Technical Collaboration Groups (TCGs) were established by the Technical Task Force of the IIRC to coordinate the input from participants from different countries and the disciplines as testified by the five background papers prepared in association with lead organization on the following topics: Business Model, Capitals, Connectivity, Materiality, Value Creation (see http://integratedreporting.org/resource/background-papers/). In April 2013, the Consultation Draft of the Integrated Reporting Framework was published and a further three-month period of consultation was started between April and July 2013. Finally, in December 2013 the international <IR> framework has been released.

The new phase, commenced in 2014, has been defined by the IIRC in its strategic plan (2014–2017) as the "breakthrough phase" in which a broader adoption of the Framework is expected, involving the market testing.

3.4.2.2 The Content of the <IR> Integrated Reporting Framework

The Framework is principle-based and structured into the following sections:

- Definition of Integrated Report and Fundamental Concept;
- Guiding Principles (see Table 3.3);
- Content Elements (see Table 3.4).

The <IR> framework is principle-based in order to be easily adaptable to different sectors and markets. However, guidelines are provided to support the adoption and favour comparability.

The guiding principles are mandatory. However, their application requires some decisions about how to balance different principles (e.g. conciseness vs. completeness).

Table 3.3 Guiding principles of integrated reporting (IIRC 2013: 5)

• *Strategic focus and future orientation*: An integrated report should provide insight into the organization's strategy, and how it relates to the organization's ability to create value in the short, medium and long term, and to its use of and effects on the capitals.
• *Connectivity of information*: An integrated report should show a holistic picture of the combination, interrelatedness and dependencies between the factors that affect the organization's ability to create value over time.
• *Stakeholder relationships*: An integrated report should provide insight into the nature and quality of the organization's relationships with its key stakeholders, including how and to what extent the organization understands, takes into account and responds to their legitimate needs and interests.
• *Materiality*: An integrated report should disclose information about matters that substantively affect the organization's ability to create value over the short, medium and long term
• *Conciseness*: An integrated report should be concise.
• *Reliability and completeness*: An integrated report should include all material matters, both positive and negative, in a balanced way and without material error.
• *Consistency and comparability*: The information in an integrated report should be presented: (a) on a basis that is consistent over time; and (b) in a way that enables comparison with other organizations to the extent it is material to the organization's own ability to create value over time.

Table 3.4 Content elements of integrated reporting (IIRC 2013: 5)

• *Organizational overview and external environment*: What does the organization do and what are the circumstances under which it operates?
• *Governance*: How does the organization's governance structure support its ability to create value in the short, medium and long term?
• *Business model*: What is the organization's business model?
• *Risks and opportunities*: What are the specific risks and opportunities that affect the organization's ability to create value over the short, medium and long term, and how is the organization dealing with them?
• *Strategy and resource allocation*: Where does the organization want to go and how does it intend to get there?
• *Performance*: To what extent has the organization achieved its strategic objectives for the period and what are its outcomes in terms of effects on the capitals?
• *Outlook*: What challenges and uncertainties is the organization likely to encounter in pursuing its strategy, and what are the potential implications for its business model and future performance?
• *Basis of presentation*: How does the organization determine what matters to include in the integrated report and how are such matters quantified or evaluated?

As a principle-based framework, and also to allow flexibility, the <IR> Framework presents the content elements in the form of questions that have to be addressed simultaneously, as they are linked each other. This approach allows the single organization to better represent its own activities and the value creation process.

These eight principles and the related questions are presented in the following Table 3.4.

Highlighting the aim of maintaining flexibility and to allow a performance measurement process coherent with the specific features of each organization, the framework does not require specific KPIs or even their adoption:

"KPIs that combine financial measures with other components (e.g., the ratio of greenhouse gas emissions to sales) or narrative that explains the financial implications of significant effects on other capitals and other causal relationships (e.g., expected revenue growth resulting from efforts to enhance human capital) may be used to demonstrate the connectivity of financial performance with performance regarding other capitals. In some cases, this may also include monetizing certain effects on the capitals (e.g., carbon emissions and water use)" (<IR> framework: 28).

For a better understanding of the approach and the philosophy underpinning the Framework, three fundamental concepts, upon which the inner process is grounded, deserve close attention: the concept of value creation, the capital to be reported and the value creation process.

The *concept of value creation* adopted in the <IR> framework is strongly connected to concepts and theories discussed in the first chapter. In fact, the ultimate idea is that "value is not created by or within an organization alone. It is:

- Influenced by the external environment
- Created through relationships with stakeholders
- Dependent on various resources" (IIRC 2013: p. 10).

The core of the approach followed by the IIRC lies in the value creation: each organisation, while managing its activities, absorbs different "capitals" and, at the end of the production process, it releases some output, producing some outcome. All the activities within an organization (e.g. customer satisfaction, suppliers' relationship, reputation, etc.) have an impact on the value creation, even if not necessarily in the short term. The created value, which will be reconnected to the capitals initially employed, is not relevant only for the organization itself and its stakeholders, but also for a large plethora of stakeholders and the environment at large. As stated in the Framework, "the ability of an organization to create value for itself is linked to the value it creates for others" (IIRC: 4). Even the activities that are not usually directly linked to value creation, nonetheless impact on the overall results of a firm, especially in the long term. Therefore, the integrated report should include all information relating to its activities that are material in the ability to create value in the long-term.

The other constitutive concept of the framework is "*capitals*", which the IIRC defines as "stocks of value that are increased, decreased or transformed through the activities and outputs of the organization" (IIRC 2013: 11). It comprises *financial*, *manufactured*, *intellectual*, *human*, *social* and *relationship*, and *natural*. However, organizations preparing the IR do not need to adopt this categorization. The various categories are provided because they are part of the theoretical underpinning of the value creation concept, and as a guideline for the organization in order to allow the inclusion of all forms of capital involved in the value creation process.

The *value creation process* presented in the framework is summarized in the Fig. 3.2 provided in the official IIRC guidelines. It aims at clarifying how the different components (external environment, mission and vision, governance, business model, capitals as inputs, business activities, output and outcome) are interlinked.

The *external environment* comprehends several different conditions (technological, social, environmental, etc.) and constitutes the context in which the organization operates.

The *mission* and *vision* drive activities and decisions undertaken by the organization and are related with *governance* in creating a paramount condition to encourage the value creation process of the organization.

The *business model* is at the core of the process and distinguishes the organization in the use of *inputs* and in how these are transformed, through *business activities*, in *output*s (products, services, by-products and waste) which in turn will produce some *outcome*s.

A culture of innovation in the complete process is indicated as a key element both for generating new products and services and for improving efficiency in the use of resources and for even finding alternative uses for outputs.

Summarising, the concept of value creation embedded in the <IR> framework is wider than the traditional business model, including all the 'outcomes' of the activities for each category of capitals described. It depends on the willingness to offer a long-term perspective, offering an overview of the negative or positive future outcomes.

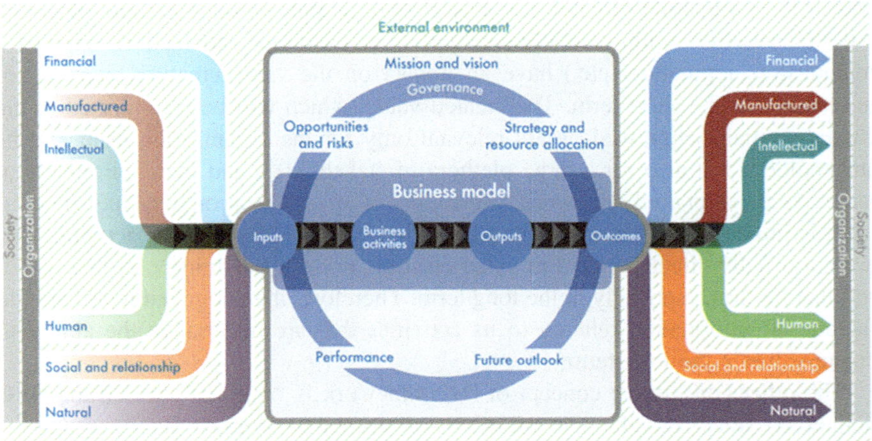

Fig. 3.2 International <IR> framework value creation process.
Source International Integrated Reporting Council, International <IR> Framework: 13

To conclude the analysis of the two main frameworks attracting the attention of scholars, consultants and organizations worldwide, a comparison of the two document as discussed in Eccles et al. (2015) is presented in the Table 3.5.

Table 3.5 Comparison between the IRC of the SA's DP and the IIRC frameworks (Eccles et al. 2015: 47)

Topic/Concept	IRC South Africa discussion paper	IIRC International <IR> Framework
Context	Corporate governance (in terms of integrity, transparency and accountability)	Value creation over time
Integrated thinking	Term not used	Core concept
Integrated report versus integrated reporting	Yes. The integrated report is the report itself, the product, while the second is the business process	The first one is the final document while the second word supports the concept of integrated thinking
Principles-based	Yes	Yes
Report Audience	Multiple stakeholders	Multiple stakeholders
Framework users	Any organization	Any organization (mainly private for-profits but adaptable to other types)
Time frame	Short, medium and long term	Short, medium and long term
Has a model for value creation?	No	Yes
Sustainability	Core to the discussion	Core to the discussion of value creation
Architecture of the framework	Three reporting principles, Eight elements, Nine steps for preparing an integrated report	Fundamental concepts, Seven guiding principles and eight content elements
Materiality	Defined by the company (in terms of issues affecting value over the short, medium and long-term) and distinguishes between financial and nonfinancial definition	Defined by the company in terms of issues that substantively affect the organization's ability to create value over the short, medium and long-term
Stakeholder engagement	Extensive	Yes, included in one of the guiding principles
Gives Guidance on how to prepare an integrated report	Yes	Yes
Discussion on how to leverage company's website	Only that it should be posted there	Web-based content and hyperlinks are mentioned
Has regulatory backing	Yes, companies that want to be listed in the Johannesburg Stock Exchange has to provide an integrated report	No
Discusses assurance	Yes	Yes, in reference of the fact that independent assurance enhances reliability

In its Directors' guide to integrated reporting Deloitte (2015a) underlines the role played by the <IR> framework in supporting organization in order to gain trust; being the IR devoted to align strategies, business models and metrics attuned to report outputs and outcomes, the IR favours transparency and accountability and, in turn, trust. This point assumes a pivotal role in public sector entities, due to their responsibility towards citizens in managing public resources.

3.5 Drawing the Path from Sustainability to Integrated Reporting

To fully understand the current state of the art in the adoption of Integrated Reporting, it is worth considering how environmental and sustainability issues are perceived nowadays. The extent of the Integrated Reporting adopted, will be presented with reference to recent surveys published by consultant firms and standard setter.

The increasing production of sustainability reports is unquestionable, and the GRI is paying a growing attention to future challenges and to the direction of corporate sustainability reporting, fostering a growing stakeholder engagement.

Figure 3.3 shows the tremendous increase in the production of corporate social responsibility reporting.

The KPMG Report (2015) recognized that organizations tend to publish an integrated report after years of Sustainability Reporting, highlighting a clear connection between the two reports. Thus, the exponential increase of organizations reporting on Sustainability (from 11 in 1999 to 5463 in 2015 according to the GRI database) can be positively interpreted in respect to the diffusion of IR.

However, as declared by Bill Murphy, Partner KPMG (KPMG 2015: 38), "While more than half of the companies surveyed now include CR information in their annual financial reports, only 11 % refer to their reports as integrated. The remainder appear to consider the inclusion of selected CR information in the financial report as adequate disclosure for investors, without moving towards a convergence of their annual and CR reports". The move towards a conscious

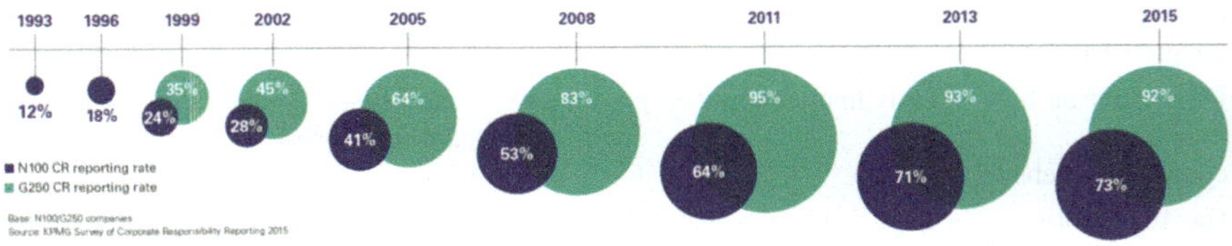

Fig. 3.3 Corporate responsibility reporting in the largest companies worldwide [N100 are the 100 largest companies in 41 countries, while G250 comprises the top 250 companies listed in the Fortune Global 500 ranking for 2014, with the 74 % of the G250 using the GRI framework (KPMG 2015: 42)].
Source KPMG (2015: 30)

adoption of IR seems to be slow. A possible positive element that pushes towards the adoption of IR can be the presence of a CSR Manager or a sustainability unit, according to results referred to by G250 companies (KPMG 2013).

Another emerging relevant element is the increasing practice to assure CSR reports, which progressively give a high relevance and trustiness to this kind of report (KPMG 2013).

The recent amendments approved by the European Parliament to the Directive 2014/95/EU, introduce the requirement for large companies (with more than 500 employees) and other entities belonging to specific sector, to disclose non-financial information (European Parliament 2014). As already discussed, a public consultation has just been concluded (April 2016) with the aim of collecting views from a large plethora of stakeholders, on non-binding guidance on the methodology for reporting of non-financial information; finally, 269 responses have been uploaded. Results show that the more relevant aspect to be addressed in an Integrated Reporting document should be materiality (most important element for 53.5 % of the respondents), usefulness (7.4 %), reliability (6.3 %) and comparability (4.0 %). However, the most interesting result which emerged from public consultation is that, in accordance with respondents, the main audience for the non-financial statement should be all users of the information (including consumers, local communities, NGOs, etc.) (49.4 %), while stakeholders are considered to be the main audience only by the 7.8 %.

Moreover, it is important to mention that IIRC and IASB in December 2014 have announced a memorandum of understanding to develop an IR framework, furtherly reinforcing the role of the IASB, which already has a seat on the board of the IIRC.

A further relevant point to consider while discussing the possible move from CSR reporting to IR is the role played by relevant consulting companies, especially the "big four" (Deloitte, E&Y, KPMG, and PwC), which are progressively providing their clients with methodologies attuned to favour the adoption of IR. However, they are also among the "top players" that in the comment letters sent for public consultation on the IR Framework manifested their concerns about possible duplication of information, requesting clarity on different aspects, such as to what extent is the IR a new report or merely a consolidation of existing reports (Zambon 2014). In the same vein, banks and insurance companies have expressed similar concerns about the duplication of efforts in the disclosure. A more general concern has been also expressed in regard to the concept of materiality, linked with the element of integration of information, and the possibility of a concrete standardization on the matter (Reuter and Messner 2015).

In accordance with the theoretical approach followed in the present work, the IR should be the result of a clear and conscious process of change started by both Board and Management concluding with the IR. In this context, IR has to be able to show the integrated-thinking approach followed by the entity in order to result in being effective and durable throughout time. To this end, it is worth noting a recent report released by the Association of Chartered Certified Accountants (ACCA 2013) and the Climate Disclosure Standards Board (CDSB). In this report, considering the different approach and methodologies in use for the preparation of IR, they state that the actual fragmentation of the landscape might mean that the discipline is lost in the right direction.

To conclude, although a clear map defining the state of the art of the experience of IR cannot be traced thus far, it is undeniably a growing attention to this encompassing tool. It is testified not only by the increasing number of integrated and sustainability reports published, but most and foremost by the rise in quality, and increasing interest by national and supranational institutions and organizations who support the disclosure of nonfinancial information (Deloitte 2015b).

3.6 Challenges of Integrated Reporting

To complete the overview on Integrated Reporting that this chapter offers are the challenges as well as some criticisms relating to integrated reporting which have emerged among scholars as well as from first experiences.

A first question is about "why" the introduction of IR: why should an organization be interested in publishing an integrated reporting?

One of the main criticisms raised in regard to IR is its relationship with other forms of reporting and the risk of an overlapping.

It is still too early to clarify this grey area, however, results have emerged by some surveys conducted by standard setters and consulting companies that can support the discussion. Some motivations appeared in favour of the adoption of IR and to a certain extent similarly to what happens with the introduction of CSR reports: to combine financial and non-financial information into a sole report (ACCA 2012a, b); to increase sustainability awareness with investors and customers, improve transparency and data accuracy, enhance brand and reputation (E&Y and GreenBiz 2013); to balance the demands for transparency against legal risk and other considerations in releasing such information (E&Y and GreenBiz 2013).

Other benefits that are more strictly attributable to IR are business model innovation, product innovation and new revenue streams are perceived as having direct benefits, as well as reduced cost of capital, growing employee engagement, improving security and quality of supply (PwC 2015).

Additionally, according to a PwC report (2015) companies that have already undertaken the road of IR demonstrate better understanding of business opportunities and risks (65 %), improvements in decision making (79 %) and more collaborative thinking about targets and goals by the board and strategy departments (78 %).

A document published by the IIRC based on a survey in 2015 reports a positive benefit in relation with institutional investors and financial analysts. Moreover, companies believe that IR offers a better understanding of the organization's strategy to providers of financial capital, allowing them to have a greater confidence in the long-term viability of business models (IIRC 2015).

A research made by Serafeim (2015) demonstrated that companies with more IR have a more long-term investor base. Moreover he found that investors activism on sustainability issues lead companies to practice more IR.

There are also criticisms, particularly the IIRC reports problems related to comparability and the correct connectivity between different sets of information, leading towards a concrete materiality (IIRC 2015). Moreover, The EY report (2015a, b) shows that between investors who do not use non-financial information, the 46 % consider it to be unclear as to whether this information is material or has financial impact, and more than 28 % consider non-financial information inconsistent, unavailable or not verified, demonstrating that there is still some resistance and doubt against this data.

A further risk, highlighted in the PwC report (2014) is a possible overflow of information due to a propensity to incorporate marketing information rather than give an in-depth picture on how the business really plans to create value. An additional risk foreshadow is "that reporting appeared more like a compliance exercise than a compelling and authentic story that covers the content elements and adopts the principles in their own words, in a way that is easily understood" (PwC 2014). The same report calls for broadening horizons, focusing on the ability to create value in the future, as well as for a clear alignment between strategy, KPI and incentive schemes, reinforcing the connection between key activities and performance.

Some scholars have indicated criticisms toward the IR and the framework recently issued, some others demonstrate a more enthusiastic approach to the IR. In this strand, Eccles and Krzus (2010b) consider that IR gives more clarity about relationships and commitments, supporting the organization in identifying essential financial and nonfinancial metrics in its specific sector and which strategy it should follow to achieve its objectives. Thus, it turns out to be a better decision-making process, ensuring a better coordination among units within the organization. For the same authors, an organization that perceives the benefits of internal cooperation, will look for the same cooperation externally, and this process will result, in turn, to be a better stakeholder engagement and creation of opportunities to make stakeholders' and shareholders' interests converge. They also clarify that IR can support companies in reducing reputational risk, as confirmed also by the study of Deloitte (2014). Other scholars, similarly to what consultant companies reveal, demonstrate a correlation between IR reports (or even sustainability reports) and access to financial resources (Cheng et al. 2014), while Serafeim (2015), as already highlighted, demonstrates the increase in the number of long-term investors. Jensen and Berg (2012) have also demonstrated the likelihood that IR companies can originate mainly from countries with higher investor protection.

From a different perspective, other scholars discuss that whilst companies' interest in addressing sustainability and ecological issues are moving quickly, the approach proposed by the IIRC is embedded within the business model, framed in social and environmental reporting. Adopting IR would support only organizations with weak forms of social and environmental reporting, while it results in being ineffective for those who need to examine, through a critical lens, the way of thinking, theories, appraisal techniques and reporting practices, which remain designed to satisfy the interest of capital providers rather than public interests (Milne and Gray 2013; Brown and Dillard 2014). Moreover, following Reuter and Messner (2015) the famous Young's (2003) there are concerns that there is more rhetoric than substance in standard-setters' reference to "user needs" and it might also be referred to the IR framework.

A further risk, particularly relevant for State-Owned Enterprises (SOE) providing public services holding a monopoly, has been highlighted by Frías-Aceituno et al. (2013). For the authors, companies operating under a monopoly constraint are less likely to publish IR that present relevant information for decision taking.

A further concern regards the concrete ability of IR in reducing reporting length and complexity, despite the required conciseness (Rowbottom and Locke 2016) stated in the IR framework.

Stubbs and Higgins (2014) and Higgins et al. (2014) discuss the possibility of IR introducing radical change in organisational thinking. In particular, Higgins et al. (2014) interviewed 15 Australian Managers belonging to a group of early adopters, in order to explore the sense-making processes, in the context of institutional theory. The authors identified strategic motivations as the rationale for undertaking IR. However, they found little radical changes, and call for further research verifying if the rhetoric signifiers of "shared value", "capital", "stewardship" and "materiality" do offer opportunities for effecting radical change in organisational activities.

The work of Robertson and Samy (2015) adds a further relevant element, in practice, about the introduction of IR. The authors discuss how IR fits in with the other national and international standard setting bodies, and, rather than adopting an internal perspective, they demonstrate that managers still perceive a weak linkage between financial and non-financial information, thus resulting in favour of the adoption of IR. It can be questioned that this would be a result strictly connected to the state of early adopters, whom have received a benefit in term of better reputation from the introduction of IR (Steyn 2014). Robertson and Samy (2015), as well as Adams (2015), also state clearly their concern for the complexity of the capital measurement concept that should assign a value to social and relation capital.

All in all, the road for the definitive consensus around the content, the process, the format and, above all, the concrete usefulness of IR seems to be still long.

Scholars play a critical role toward the indiscriminate promotion of any form of corporate reporting emerging in practice. In the case of IR they can act as a promoter of the adoption of an integrated-thinking approach by managers and directors, and that would constitute the key-element to ensure the preparation of sound information within the IR. As things stand, there seems to emerge a need to investigate the organization reaction to the adoption, development and diffusion of IR, especially with in-depth case-studies, looking for the organizational changes embedded in the construction of IR.

References

Abdel-Khalik R (2011) Fair value accounting and stewardship. Acc Perspect 9:253–269
Abeysekera I (2013) A template for integrated reporting. J Intellect Capital 14(2):227–245
Abhayawansa S (2014) A review of guidelines and frameworks on external reporting of intellectual capital. J Intellect Capital 15(1):100–141
ACCA (2012a) Re-assessing the value of corporate reporting. ACCA Global, London
ACCA (2012b) Reporting pre- and post-king III: what's the difference? Available at http://www.accaglobal.com/content/dam/acca/global/PDF-technical/integrated-reporting/tech-tp-wtd.pdf. Accessed 20 March 2016
ACCA (2013) Understanding investors: directions for corporate reporting. Available at http://www.accaglobal.com/content/dam/acca/global/PDF-technical/financial-reporting/pol-afb-ui02.pdf. Accessed 16th May 2016
Adams CA (2004) The ethical, social and environmental reporting-performance portrayal gap. Acc Auditing Accountability J 17(5):731–757
Adams CA (2015) The international integrated reporting council: a call to action. Crit Perspect Acc 27:23–28
Aguilera RV (2005) Corporate governance and director accountability: an institutional comparative perspective. Br J Manage 16:S39–S53
Amir E, Lev B (1996) Value-relevance of nonfinancial information: the wireless communications industry. J Acc Econ 22(1):3–30
Ball A, Grubnic S, Birchall J (2014) Sustainability accounting and accountability in the public sector. In: Bebbington J, Unerman J, O'Dwyer B (eds) Sustainability accounting and accountability, Routledge, pp 176–196
Bartocci L, Picciaia F (2013) Towards integrated reporting in the public sector. In: Busco C, Frigo ML, Riccaboni A, Quattrone P (eds) Integrated reporting: concepts and cases that redefine corporate accountability, Springer Science & Business Media, Springer International Publishing, Switzerland, pp 191–204
Beattie V, Smith SJ (2013) Value creation and business models: refocusing the intellectual capital debate. Br Acc Rev 45(4):243–254
Bebbington J, Unerman J, O'Dwyer B (2014) Sustainability accounting and accountability. Routledge, New York
Bendell J, Miller A, Wortmann K (2011) Public policies for scaling corporate responsibility standards. Sustain Acc Manage Policy J 2(2):263–293
Botosan C (1997) Disclosure level and the cost of equity capital. Acc Rev 72(3):323–349
Bouwman MJ, Frishkoff PA, Frishkoff P (1987) How do financial analysts make decisions? a process model of the investment screening decision. Acc Organ Soc 12(1):1–29
Brown J, Dillard J (2014) Integrated reporting: on the need for broadening out and opening up. Acc Auditing Accountability J 27(7):1120–1156
Busco C, Frigo ML, Riccaboni A, Quattrone P (2013) Towards integrated reporting: concepts, elements and principles. In: Busco C, Frigo ML, Riccaboni A, Quattrone P (eds) Integrated reporting: concepts and cases that redefine corporate accountability, Springer Science & Business Media, Springer International Publishing, Switzerland, pp 3–18
Cheng B, Ioannou I, Serafeim G (2014) Corporate social responsibility and access to finance. Strateg Manage J 35(1):1–23
Committee on the Financial Aspects of Corporate Governance (1992) Report with code of best practice [Cadbury report]. Gee Publishing, London
Cooper DJ, Morgan W (2013) Meeting the evolving corporate reporting needs of government and society. Acc Bus Res 43(4):418–441
de Villiers C, Rinaldi L, Unerman J (2014) Integrated reporting: insights, gaps and an agenda for future research. Acc Auditing Accountability J 27(7):1042–1067

Deegan C, Rankin M, Tobin J (2002) An examination of the corporate social and environmental disclosures of BHP from 1983–1997: a test of legitimacy theory. Acc Auditing Accountability J 15(3):312–343
Deloitte (2014) 2014 global survey on reputation risk [online]. Available from http://www2.deloitte.com/content/dam/Deloitte/global/Documents/Governance-Risk-Compliance/gx_grc_Reputation@Risk%20survey%20report_FINAL.pdf. Accessed 20 March 2016
Deloitte (2015a) A directors' guide to integrated reporting [online]. Available from http://www2.deloitte.com/content/dam/Deloitte/na/Documents/audit/na_za_Directors_Guide_on_Integrated_Reporting.pdf. Accessed 17 March 2015
Deloitte (2015b) Integrated reporting as a driver for integrated thinking? Available at https://www2.deloitte.com/content/dam/Deloitte/nl/Documents/risk/deloitte-nl-risk-integrated-reporting-a-driver-for-integrated-thinking.pdf. Accessed 20 March 2016
Druckman P, Fries J (2010) Integrated reporting: the future of corporate reporting? In: Eccles RG, Cheng B, Saaltzman D (eds) The landscape of integrated reporting, The president and fellows of Harvard College, Massachusetts, pp 81–85
Dumay J, Guthrie J, Puntillo P (2015) IC and public sector: a structured literature review. J Intellect Capital 16(2):267–284
Eccles RG, Krzus MP (2010a) One report: integrated reporting for a sustainable society. Wiley, USA
Eccles RG, Krzus MP (2010b) Integrated reporting for a sustainable strategy. Financ Executive 26 (2):28–33
Eccles RG, Krzus MP (with Sidney Ribot) (2015) The integrated reporting movement: meaning, momentum, motives, and materiality. Wiley, New Jersey
Eccles RG, Serafeim G (2014) Corporate and integrated reporting: a functional perspective. Working paper, Harvard Business School, pp 14–094
EFRAG, ANC, FRC (2012) Towards a disclosure framework for the notes. EFRAG, Brussels
Ernest & Young (EY) (2015a) Tomorrow's investment rules 2.0 emerging risk and stranded assets have investors looking for more from nonfinancial reporting. http://www.ey.com/Publication/vwLUAssets/EY-tomorrows-investment-rules-2/$FILE/EY-tomorrows-investment-rules-2.0.pdf. Accessed 8 May 2016
Ernest & Young (EY) (2015b) Excellence in integrated reporting awards. http://www.ey.com/Publication/vwLUAssets/ey-excellence-in-integrated-reporting-awards-2015/$FILE/ey-excellence-in-integrated-reporting-awards-2015.pdf. Accessed 19 March 2016
European Parliament (2014) Directive 2014/95/EU of the European Parliament and of the Council of 22 October 2014 amending Directive 2013/34/EU as regards disclosure of non-financial and diversity information by certain large undertakings and groups. Off J Eur Union (15/11/2014). http://eur-lex.europa.eu/legal-content/EN/TXT/?uri=uriserv:OJ.L_.2014.330.01.0001.01.ENG. Accessed 22 May 2016
EY, GreenBiz (2013) 2013 six growing trends in corporate sustainability [online]. Available from http://www.ey.com/Publication/vwLUAssets/Six_growing_trends_in_corporate_sustainability_2013/$FILE/Six_growing_trends_in_corporate_sustainability_2013.pdf. Accessed 16th May 2016
Farneti F, Guthrie J (2009) Sustainability reporting by Australian public sector organisations: why they report. Acc Forum 33(2):89–98
Fasan M (2013) Annual reports, sustainability reports and integrated reports: trends in corporate disclosure. In: Busco C, Frigo ML, Riccaboni A, Quattrone P (eds) Integrated reporting: concepts and cases that redefine corporate accountability, Springer Science & Business Media, Springer International Publishing, Switzerland, pp 41–57
FASB (2015) Notes to financial statements (Topic 235): assessing whether disclosures are material
Ferenhof HA, Durst S, Zaniboni Bialecki M, Selig PM (2015) Intellectual capital dimensions: state of the art in 2014. J Intellect Capital 16(1):58–100
Frías-Aceituno JV, Rodríguez-Ariza L, García-Sánchez IM (2013) Is integrated reporting determined by a country's legal system? An exploratory study. J Clean Prod 44:45–55

Gray R (2001) Thirty years of social accounting, reporting and auditing: what (if anything) have we learnt? Bus Ethics A Eur Rev 10(1):9–15

Gray R, Owen D, Maunders K (1988) Corporate social reporting: emerging trends in accountability and the social contract. Acc Auditing Accountability J 1(1):6–20

GRI (Global Reporting Initiative) (2005) Sector supplement for public agencies, Amsterdam

GRI (Global Reporting Initiative) (2013) The sustainability content of integrated reports—a survey of pioneers. Research and development series, Amsterdam

GRI (Global Reporting Initiative) (2016) The next era of corporate disclosure: digital, responsible, interactive. https://www.globalreporting.org/resourcelibrary/The-Next-Era-of-Corporate-Disclosure.pdf. Accessed 16 June 2016

Grimmelikhuijsen S, Porumbescu G, Hong B, Im T (2013) The effect of transparency on trust in government: a cross-national comparative experiment. Public Adm Rev 73(4):575–586

Guthrie J (2001) The management, measurement and the reporting of intellectual capital. J Intellect Capital 2(1):27–41

Guthrie J, Farneti F (2008) GRI sustainability reporting by Australian public sector organizations. Public Money Manage 28(6):361–366

Guthrie J, Parker LD (1989) Corporate social reporting: a rebuttal of legitimacy theory. Acc Bus Res 19(76):343–352

Haxhi I, Aguilera RV (2015) Corporate governance through codes. Wiley Encycl Manage 6:1–3

Higgins C, Stubbs W, Love T (2014) Walking the talk(s): organisational narratives of integrated reporting. Acc Auditing Accountability J 27(7):1090–1119

IASB (2010) Conceptual framework for financial reporting

IIRC (2013) International <IR> framework. http://integratedreporting.org/resource/international-ir-framework/. Accessed 12th July 2016

IIRC (2015) Creating value: integrated reporting <IR> and investor benefits. Available at http://integratedreporting.org/wp-content/uploads/2015/12/Creating-Value-Integrated-Reporting-and-investor-benefits.pdf. Accessed 16th May 2016

IIRC Database. http://examples.integratedreporting.org/search?page_num=1&x=38&y=15&organisation_ type=&organisation_region=&organisation_industry=10&report_type=&report_year=&fragment_fundamental=&fragment_content. Accessed 19 March 2016

IPSASB (2014) The conceptual framework for general purpose financial reporting by public sector entities (IFAC)

IRC of SA (2011) Discussion paper of the framework for integrated reporting and the integrated report discussion paper. Available at http://www.sustainabilitysa.org/Portals/0/IRC%20of%20SA%20Integrated%20Reporting%20Guide%20Jan%2011.pdf. Accessed 20 March 2016

Jensen JC, Berg N (2012) Determinants of traditional sustainability reporting versus integrated reporting: an institutionalist approach. Bus Strategy Environ 21(5):299–316

Jensen MC, Meckling WH (1976) Theory of the firm: managerial behavior, agency costs and ownership structure. J Financ Econom 3(4):305–360

Kolk A (2008) Sustainability, accountability and corporate governance: exploring multinationals' reporting practices. Bus Strategy Environ 17(1):1–15

KPMG (2010) Integrated reporting—closing the loop of strategy. http://www.kpmg.com/GR/en/IssuesAndInsights/ArticlesPublications/Sustainability/Pages/Sustainable-Insight-April-2010.aspx. Accessed 19 March 2016

KPMG (2013) The KPMG survey of corporate responsibility reporting 2013. Available at https://www.kpmg.com/Global/en/IssuesAndInsights/ArticlesPublications/corporate-responsibility/Documents/corporate-responsibility-reporting-survey-2013-exec-summary.pdf. Accessed 19 March 2016

KPMG (2015) The KPMG survey of corporate responsibility reporting 2015. Available at http://www.kpmg.com/cn/en/issuesandinsights/articlespublications/pages/kpmg-survey-of-corporate-responsibility-reporting-2015-o-201511.aspx. Accessed 19 March 2016

Lang MH, Lundholm RJ (1996) Corporate disclosure policy and analyst behavior. Acc Rev 71(4):467–492

Leung S, Parker L, Courtis J (2015) Impression management through minimal narrative disclosure in annual reports. Br Acc Rev 47(3):275–289
Mammatt J (2009) Integrated sustainability reporting and assurance. Proceedings for CIS corporate governance conference, Johannesburg
Massaro M, Dumay J, Garlatti A (2015) Public sector knowledge management: a structured literature review. J Knowl Manage 19(3):530–558
MERITUM Project (2002) Guidelines for managing and reporting on intangibles (Intellectual capital report). European Commission, Madrid
Milne MJ, Gray R (2013) W(h)ither ecology? the triple bottom line, the global reporting initiative, and corporate sustainability reporting. J Bus Ethics 118(1):13–29
O'Connell V (2007) Reflections on stewardship reporting. Acc Horiz 21(2):215–227
PwC (2014) Learning from early adopters of integrated reporting five themes to drive improvement. Available at http://www.pwc.com/gx/en/audit-services/publications/assets/pwc-learning-from-early-adopters-of-integrated-reporting.pdf
PwC (2015) Implementing integrated reporting. Available at https://www.pwc.com/gx/en/audit-services/publications/assets/pwc-ir-practical-guide.pdf. Accessed 19 March 2016
PwC South Africa (2010) King III—chapter 9: integrated reporting and disclosure. http://www.pwc.co.za/en/king3/integrated-reporting-and-disclosure.html. Accessed 19 March 2016
Reuter M, Messner M (2015) Lobbying on the integrated reporting framework: an analysis of comment letters to the 2011 discussion paper of the IIRC. Acc Auditing Accountability J 28 (3):365–402
Robertson FA, Samy M (2015) Factors affecting the diffusion of integrated reporting–a UK FTSE 100 perspective. Sustain Acc Manage Policy J 6(2):190–223
Rowbottom N, Locke J (2016) The emergence of <IR>. Acc Bus Res 46(1):83–115
Serafeim G (2015) Integrated reporting and investor clientele. J Appl Corp Finance 27(2):34–51
Solomon JF, Solomon A (2006) Private social, ethical and environmental disclosure. Acc Auditing Accountability J 19(4):564–591
Solstice Sustainability Works, Inc. (2005) Integrated reporting: issues and implications for reporters. https://www.vancity.com/lang/fr/SharedContent/documents/IntegratedReporting.pdf. Accessed 20 Jan 2016
Steyn M (2014) Organisational benefits and implementation challenges of mandatory integrated reporting: perspectives of senior executives at South African listed companies. Sustain Acc Manage Policy J 5(4):476–503
Stubbs W, Higgins C (2014) Integrated reporting and internal mechanisms of change. Acc Auditing Accountability J 27(7):1068–1089
United Nation Global Compact (2014) Guide to corporate sustainability. Shaping a sustainable future. https://www.unglobalcompact.org/docs/publications/UN_Global_Compact_Guide_to_Corporate_Sustainability.pdf. Accessed 15 May 2016
VanWensen K, BroerW, Klein J, Knopf J (2011) The state of play in sustainability reporting in the European Union 2010. Brussels, Belgium
Vergoossen RG (1993) The use and perceived importance of annual reports by investment analysts in the Netherlands. European Acc Rev 2(2):219–244
Watts RL (1977) Corporate financial statements, a product of the market and political processes. Australian J Manage 2(1):53–75
White AL (2005) New wine, new bottles: the rise of non-financial reporting. Bus Brief Bus Soc Responsib 20
Young JJ (2003) Constructing, persuading and silencing: the rhetoric of accounting standards. Acc Organ Soc 28(6):621–638
Zambon S (2014) An analysis of the comment letters by the top 50 players on the key questions of the IIRC public consultation. WICI Europe/WICI Italy, Available at http://www.wici-global.com/wp-content/uploads/2014/07/Analysis-of-the-Comment-Letters-to-IIRC-CD-by-Top-50-Players-on-key-questions.pdf. Accessed 16 May 2016

Chapter 4
Accounting Change and Integrated Reporting in Practice: The Case of Hera

Abstract The chapter intends to verify, through a case study on the progressive implementation of the IR, the way in which the intra organizational dynamics play a key role in the evolution of management accounting change and impacts on the overall result and success of the change process. The Hera Group case study intends to grasp a useful "lesson to learn" for other entities located in the public sector realm, that are willing to introduce the integrated thinking towards the IR, in order to be more efficiently managed by key organizational actors and managers. The analysis considers both the external change, the integrated thinking and IR disclosure prepared by a public sector entity and its changes over time, as well as the internal change, viewed as the progressive internalization of the integrated thinking and the path towards it. To this aim, the approach and the experience of Hera is presented, outlining features, evolution, similarities and differences of the Hera Sustainability Report with the Integrated Reporting framework, as well as the management accounting change towards the institutionalization of the integrated thinking. This case study is an important and informative example of how integrated reporting is a useful tool for governing an organization such as Hera, operating in the public services sector and owned by both public administrations and private investors.

Keywords Integrated reporting · Sustainability reporting · Management accounting change · Hera · Public sector organizations · Case study

4.1 The Path Towards Integrated Reporting in Practice

To answer the rising demand of information needs by different stakeholders a new tool is receiving attention by both standard setters and scholars, that of Integrated Reporting (IR). IR combines the presentation of financial, social and environmental information in one report (see for all Eccles and Krzus 2010). In the raising

---

This chapter was written by Rebecca L. Orelli.

E. Katsikas et al., *Towards Integrated Reporting*,
SpringerBriefs in Accounting, DOI 10.1007/978-3-319-47235-5_4

complexity of the environment in which organizations must operate, IR seems to be one of the most challenging and demanding tasks for any organization.

IR should be the result of the "integrated thinking" of an organization (Adams 2015), and it involves a process of management accounting change for the organization. In this vein, the disclosure related to IR is the final step of a progressive institutionalization process of integrated thinking (Higgins et al. 2014).

IR was initially born and developed in the private domain, and recently it expanded into the public sector. The present chapter aims at ascertain the extent to which IR can answer the information needs of a public sector entity's stakeholders and the process through which this process can be successful in practice. Even if the path towards the integrated thinking and IR is entity based, the anticipated research could be able to shed light on steps and tips towards the integrated thinking.

The proposed analysis considers both the external change, the integrated thinking and IR disclosure prepared by a public sector entity and its changes over time, as well as the internal change, viewed as the progressive internalization of integrated thinking and the path towards it.

More specifically, the present study intends to verify, through a case-study on the progressive implementation of the IR, the way in which the intra organizational dynamics play a key role in the evolution of management accounting change and impacts on the overall result and success of the change process.

The discussion of the previous chapters highlights the complexity of the management accounting change process and shows there is a need for relevant skills and expertise in order for the change to be successfully adopted in each phase of the change process. To understand the management accounting change process in practice more in depth, the present chapter contributes to the provision of knowledge related to the phenomenon of accounting change in a specific case setting.

The Hera Group case study intends to grasp a useful "lesson to learn" for other entities located in the public sector realm, that are willing to introduce the integrated thinking towards the IR, in order to be more efficiently managed by key organizational actors and managers. To this aim, the present chapter analyses the approach and the experience of Hera, outlining features, evolution, similarities and differences of the Hera Sustainability Report with the Integrated Reporting framework, as well as the management accounting change towards the institutionalization of the integrated thinking. This case study is an important and informative example of how integrated reporting is a useful tool for governing an organization such as Hera, operating in the public services sector and owned by both public administrations and private investors.

4.2 Methodology

As already stated, the aim of the chapter is to deeply understand in practice the change process towards the introduction of integrated thinking and IR in the public sector. To this aim, it should be considered, both the external change, the final output of the integrated thinking and IR disclosure prepared by a public sector entity and its changes over time, as well as the internal change, viewed as the way in which the intra organizational dynamics impact on the overall result of the change process.

For the purpose of the study, the use of a case study is particularly fitting. The case study can be defined as research methodology that focuses on understanding the dynamics in a management situation (Eisenhardt 1989). It is an empirical methodology 'that investigates a contemporary phenomenon within its real-life context when the boundaries between phenomena are not clearly evident and in which multiple sources of evidence are used' (Yin 1989, p. 23). The case study allows the researchers to develop an in depth understanding of complex phenomena and causation in practice (Yin 1994; Bennett and Elman 2006).

A single case study might be useful for a variety of purposes. As Lincoln and Guba (1985) and Guba and Lincoln (2005) suggest, a case study offers working hypotheses whereby the appropriateness for understanding other cases (that is its transferability) can only be assessed by comparing the similarities between the source case (the studied organization) and target cases (other organizations). The same authors highlight the limits in drawing inferences about the generality of findings from a case study.

The selection of the case study is based on the following elements: the presence of long and consolidated experiences in reporting (both financial and non-financial), an organization in the public domain, and the availability of the organization to disclose further information if needed. Therefore, the Hera Group was selected for the analysis, satisfying the abovementioned requirements. In 2012 other authors (Ruggiero and Mofardini 2013: 313–330) selected Hera as best practice in the field of integrated reporting, confirming the relevance of the organization under the IR perspective.

As for the primary sources used in the case analysis, the documents collected fall into the following categories: financial statements, documents published on many websites, code of ethics, and sustainability reporting.

The case study presentation is articulated in three steps, following the methodology used to investigate the case: the construction of an event history database, the gap analysis deriving from the comparison of the Hera Sustainability Report with the standard given by the Integrated Reporting framework over time, and the perception of the people involved in the management accounting change process.

4.2.1 Event History Database

For the development of the case, the first step was represented by the construction of an event history database (Van de Ven and Poole 2005), built up by ordering chronologically the main actions and facts relevant to the introduction of integrated thinking and IR, and triangulating different sources to ensure convergence of data.

This has allowed the reconstruction of 'who did what and when' and it is the basis of the chronology of events presented. In reconstructing the time-line we have tried to understand what events had led to the decision to introduce and progress the sustainability and subsequently the integrated thinking in the organization. It also helped to clarify by whom they had been taken forward, because of different actions, and how.

As argued by Brown and Jones (1998) also the chronology of events is in fact based, at least in part, on an ex post reconstruction and the partial accounts contained in the documents and interviews. The analysis was then developed by comparing the various sources of narratives and assessing the accuracy and internal consistency (Eisenhardt and Graebner 2007).

4.2.2 Gap Analysis Between the Documents and the Standard

To analyse features, evolution, and the similarities and differences of the Hera Sustainability Report with the Integrated Reporting framework, we made use of data collection focused primarily on documentary sources, namely all the sustainability reports of Hera between 2003 and 2015 and the IR framework.

A deductive research approach has been used because it enables to test the IR framework with the target organization current reporting system. In fact, through a deductive approach, a theoretical or conceptual framework is developed and then it is tested using the appropriate data (Van der Stede 2014).

The gap analysis was conducted by developing a framework, collecting data and testing the framework, with the calculation of a level of adherence to the framework.

The framework used to perform the analysis is based on Eccles et al. (2015). It consists of a simple structure to select best practices of integrated reporting. Taking that structure as a starting point and the IR framework as the main source of reference, it is possible to identify the presence of essential features for each content element and guiding principles of the IR.

Starting from described framework, it is possible to articulate an extensive list of features essential to an integrated report. That features can be subsequently used to perform the case analysis.

For what concerns the Guiding Principles of the IR framework (IIRC 2013), a total of 21 qualifying features were identified, as shown in Table 4.1.

Furthermore, the eight Content Elements were all included in the analysis (Table 4.2). For this group of content elements, 51 qualifying features were identified based on the same documents previously mentioned. In total, a set of 72 qualifying features were grouped into a framework to check the level of adherence of the Sustainability report of Hera to the integrated report according with the IR framework (IIRC 2013).

Table 4.1 Operationalization of the guiding principles

Guiding principles				
	Reference in the IR framework	Number[a]	Description	
Strategic focus and future orientation	Principle 3A p. 16	3.3	Explain how the company plans to use "the capitals" and the impact of business activities on the capitals	1
		4.27–4.28	Explain the time frames (short-, medium-, and long-term) associated with strategic objectives	2
		4.29	Explain the strategic importance of material risks and opportunities in the discussion of business strategy	3
Connectivity of information	Principle 3B p. 16	3.6–3.9	Link and explain the relationships between the content elements	4
		3.8 and 4.32	Explain how financial and nonfinancial performance impact each other	5
Stakeholder relationships	Principle 3C p. 17	3.34	Have the stakeholders been involved in the definition of the material issues?	6
		4.7	Have the needs and expectation of the stakeholders been considered in the definition of the external environment?	7
		4.13	Have the stakeholders been identified in the definition of the business model?	8
		4.29	Does the organization activate stakeholder engagement activities?	9
		4.29	If yes in the previous question. Are the inputs used in the definition of the strategy?	10
Materiality	Principle 3D p. 18	3.17–3.18 and 3.21–23	Explain material risks and opportunities in greater detail, especially in terms of known or potential effects on financial, environmental, social, or governance performance	11
		3.18 and 3.24–27	Identify the time frames (short-, medium-, and long-term) associated with material risk and opportunities	12
		3.18 and 3.28	Prioritize material risks and opportunities based on their magnitude/importance	13
		Chapter 5	Prioritize the perspectives of stakeholders consulted	14
		Chapter 5	Explain the role of the board of directors in the materiality process	15

(continued)

Table 4.1 (continued)

Guiding principles	Reference in the IR framework	Number[a]	Description	
Conciseness	Principle 3E p. 21	3.36–3.37	Information includes sufficient context to understand the organization's strategy, governance, performance and prospects without being burdened with less relevant information	16
		3.38	There is a balance between conciseness and the other Guiding Principles, particularly completeness and comparability	17
Reliability and completeness	Principle 3F p. 21	3.40	Are there mechanisms for reliability? (internal control, stakeholder engagement, external assurance etc.)	18
		3.42	Are the mechanisms explained in the report?	19
Consistency and comparability	Principle 3G p. 23	3.55	Information presented on a basis that is consistent over time	20
		3.56–3.57	Information presented in a way that enables comparison with other organizations	21

[a]*Note* The column number contains either the main reference of the IR framework, or the additional reference of Eccles et al. (2015a), Chaps. 5 and 6, as used by the same authors in Eccles et al. (2015b)

Once defined the tool of analysis, the two official reporting tools of the firm were collected, the Annual report and the Sustainability report, and thoroughly checked to identify the existence, or not, of the features included in the framework.

After having identified the key features that characterize an integrated report, the presence of these elements in the Hera current reporting tools was established. Each guiding principle and content element received the same weight out of the total, given the same importance of these components for calculating the level of coherence of the Sustainability Report of Hera with the IR framework. Lastly, the percentage of detected features was weighted over the total number of features of each component to obtain the general 'coherence level' to IR.

4.2.3 Key People Perception of Change

To analyse the internal change, viewed as the way in which the intra organizational dynamics impact on the overall result of the change process.as well as the management accounting change towards the institutionalization of the integrated

Table 4.2 Operationalization of the content elements

Content elements	Reference in the IR framework	Number[a]	Description	
Organizational overview and external environment	Element 4A p. 24	4.5	Identifies Mission and Vision	1
			Context on: culture, ethics and values	2
			Context on: ownership and operating structure	3
			Context on: principal activities and markets	4
			Context on: competitive landscape and market positioning	5
			Context on: position within the value chain	6
			Key quantitative information (e.g., the number of employees, revenue and number of countries in which the organization operates), highlighting, in particular, significant changes from prior periods	7
		4.6	Significant factors affecting the external environment and the organization's response	8
Governance	Element 4B p. 25	4.9	The organization's leadership structure, including the skills and diversity of those charged with governance and whether regulatory requirements influence the design of the governance structure	9
			Specific processes used to make strategic decisions and to establish and monitor the culture of the organization, including its attitude to risk and mechanisms for addressing integrity and ethical issues	10
			Particular actions those charged with governance have taken to influence and monitor the strategic direction of the organization and its approach to risk management	11

(continued)

Table 4.2 (continued)

Content elements	Reference in the IR framework	Number[a]	Description	
			How the organization's culture, ethics and values are reflected in its use of and effects on the capitals, including its relationships with key stakeholder	12
			Whether the organization is implementing governance practices that exceed legal requirements	13
			The responsibility those charged with governance take for promoting and enabling innovation	14
			How remuneration and incentives are linked to value creation in the short, medium and long term, including how they are linked to the organization's use of and effects on the capitals	15
Business model	Element 4C p. 25–27	Inputs 4.14	Relation between key inputs and capital to understand the resilience of the firm in creating value	16
		Inputs 4.15	Disclose only material inputs (whether owned or not)	17
		Business activities 4.16	How the organization differentiates itself in the market place	18
		Business activities 4.16	The extent to which the business model relies on revenue generation after the initial point of sale	19
		Business activities 4.16	How the organization approaches the need to innovate	20
		Business activities 4.16	How the business model has been designed to adapt to change	21
		Outputs 4.18	An integrated report identifies an organization's key products and services. There might be other outputs, such as by-products and waste (including emissions), that need to be discussed within the business model disclosure depending on their materiality	22

(continued)

Table 4.2 (continued)

Content elements				
	Reference in the IR framework	Number[a]	Description	
		Outcomes 4.19–4.20	Internal outcomes (e.g., employee morale, organizational reputation, revenue and cash flows) both positive and negative	23
		Outcomes 4.19–4.20	External outcome (e.g., customer satisfaction, tax payments, brand loyalty, and social and environmental effects) both positive and negative	24
		4.21	Disclosure of more than one business model if applicable	25
Risks and opportunities	Element 4D p. 27	4.25	The specific source of risks and opportunities, which can be internal, external or, commonly, a mix of the two	26
			The organization's assessment of the likelihood that the risk or opportunity will come to fruition and the magnitude of its effect if it does	27
			The specific steps being taken to mitigate or manage key risks or to create value from key opportunities	28
Strategy and resource allocation	Element 4E p. 27	4.28	The organization's short, medium and long term strategic objectives	29
			The strategies it has in place, or intends to implement, to achieve those strategic objectives	30
			The resource allocation plans it has to implement its strategy	31
			How it will measure achievements and target outcomes for the short, medium and long term	32
Performance	Element 4F p. 28	4.31	Quantitative indicators with respect to targets and risks and opportunities, explaining their significance, their implications, and the methods and assumptions used in compiling them	33
			The organization's effects (both positive and negative) on the capitals, including material effects on capitals up and down the value chain	34

(continued)

Table 4.2 (continued)

Content elements	Reference in the IR framework	Number[a]	Description	
			The state of key stakeholder relationships and how the organization has responded to key stakeholders' legitimate needs and interests	35
			The linkages between past and current performance, and between current performance and the organization's outlook	36
		4.32	KPIs that combine financial measures with other components (e.g., the ratio of greenhouse gas emissions to sales) or narrative that explains the financial implications of significant effects on other capitals and other causal relationships (e.g., expected revenue growth resulting from efforts to enhance human capital) may be used to demonstrate the connectivity of financial performance with performance regarding other capitals. In some cases, this may also include monetizing certain effects on the capitals (e.g., carbon emissions and water use)	37
Outlook	Element 4G p. 29	4.35	The organization's expectations about the external environment the organization is likely to face in the short, medium and long term	38
			How that will affect the organization	39
			How the organization is currently equipped to respond to the critical challenges and uncertainties that are likely to arise	40
		4.37	Implication for future financial performance: The external environment, and risks and opportunities, with an analysis of how these could affect the achievement of strategic objectives	41

(continued)

Table 4.2 (continued)

Content elements	Reference in the IR framework	Number[a]	Description	
			Implication for future financial performance: The availability, quality and affordability of capitals the organization uses or affects (e.g., the continued availability of skilled labour or natural resources), including how key relationships are managed and why they are important to the organization's ability to create value over time	42
		4.38 (Optional)	An integrated report may also provide lead indicators, KPIs or objectives, relevant information from recognized external sources, and sensitivity analyses	43
		4.39	Reference to the legal and regulatory requirements to which the organization is subject	44
Basis of preparation and presentation	Element 4H p. 29	4.42	Summary of materiality determination process	45
		4.43	Identification of reporting boundary and explanation of its determination	46
		4.47	Summary of significant frameworks and methods used to quantify and evaluate material matters	47
General reporting guidance	Element 4I p. 30	4.50–4.53	Disclosure of material matters	48
		4.54–4.55	Disclosure about the capitals	49
		4.57–4.59	Time frames for short, medium and long term	50
		4.60–4.62	Aggregation and disaggregation	51

[a]*Note* The column number contains either the main reference of the IR framework, or the additional reference of Eccles et al. (2015a), Chaps. 5 and 6, as used by the same authors in Eccles et al. (2015b)

thinking, the Armstrong (2006) model based on Kotter's one (1996) has been adopted.

Even though the initial stage of motivating/encoding of change may be successfully activated, the success of the whole process can fall in part or entirely in the next phase of managing/enacting or later on in the final stage of reproducing/institutionalizing. To assess the integrated thinking change in Hera it seems useful to consider eight steps proposed by authors to enacting actions in each step. The steps, already introduced in Chap. 2, are the following:

1. Establishing a sense of urgency.
2. Forming a powerful guiding coalition to lead the change effort.
3. Creating a vision and in turn developing strategies for achieving that vision.
4. Communicating the vision and strategies and teaching new behaviours.
5. Empowering others to act on the vision and encourage risk taking and non-traditional ideas, activities and actions.
6. Planning for and creating short-term wins.
7. Consolidating improvements and producing still more change by using increased credibility to change systems, structures and polices, hiring, promoting and developing employees.
8. Institutionalizing new approaches and developing the means to ensure leadership development and success.

To develop the analysis, all the sources available have been used, as described in the previous section. Moreover, the key person from the Hera group was invited to share their experience of introduction of sustainability in two official meetings with other organizations interested in sharing the internal feature of the integrated thinking effort. The analysis is grounded on the material produced from these meetings as well as the narratives of key Hera people on the topic.

4.3 Hera: Context and Background

The Hera Group is one of the largest multi-utility organizations operating in Italy throughout different service sectors: energy, water and waste management.

Hera was established in 2002 following the combination of 11 public service companies in Emilia-Romagna into one single multi-utility, capable of creating a proper 'public services industry' active in the sectors of the Environment (waste collection and treatment), Energy (distribution and sale of electricity and gas) and Water (waterworks, sewerage and purification).

Since the group is operating in different sectors, the portfolio enables Hera to reduce its risk (of regulation, seasonality, etc.), an important element since Hera is partially privatized and quoted on the Milan Stock Exchange.

Since 2002, Hera has embarked on a journey of constant growth, incorporating other companies active in the same areas into the Group, giving rise to the most relevant business combination that occurred in the Italian public utilities sector. The positive mergers and acquisitions contributed to double the Ebitda in a short period of time (Table 4.3 and Fig. 4.1).

Table 4.3 Hera mail financial data, Hera website, accessed 28 June 2016

Financial data (*mln €*)	*Cagr.% 02–15*	2015	2014	2013	2012	2011	2010	2009	2008	2007	2006	2005	2004	2003	2002
Revenues	*+11.7*	4487.0	4189.1	4456.9	4492.7	4105.7	3666.9	4204.2	3716.3	2863.3	2311.5	2100.5	1492.6	1221.5	1067.0
Ebitda	*+12.5*	884.4	867.8	810.2	662.1	644.8	607.3	567.3	528.3	453.4	426.7	386.4	292.5	242.5	191.9
Ebit	*+14.3*	442.2	441.2	399.7	335.5	334.5	315.4	291.3	280.7	220.6	231.3	215.7	177.3	112.8	77.6
Profit before tax	*+11.4*	307.9	304.4	299.8	213.5	221.2	205.6	162.6	188.9	142.5	179.2	189.3	147.5	88.6	75.3
Income taxes	*+8.6*	(113.5)	(124.3)	(118.1)	(79.1)	(94.5)	(63.6)	(77.6)	(78.6)	(32.6)	(79.0)	(80.5)	(61.1)	(35.6)	(38.7)
Net profit	*+13.7*	194.4	182.4	181.7	134.4	126.8	142.1	85.0	110.3	109.9	100.2	108.8	86.5	53.0	36.6
Minority profit	*+11.2*	13.9	17.6	16.8	15.7	22.2	24.8	13.9	15.5	13.7	10.1	7.4	5.5	3.6	3.5
Hera net profit	*+13.9*	180.5	164.8	164.9	118.7	104.6	117.2	71.1	94.8	96.2	90.1	101.4	81.0	49.5	33.2

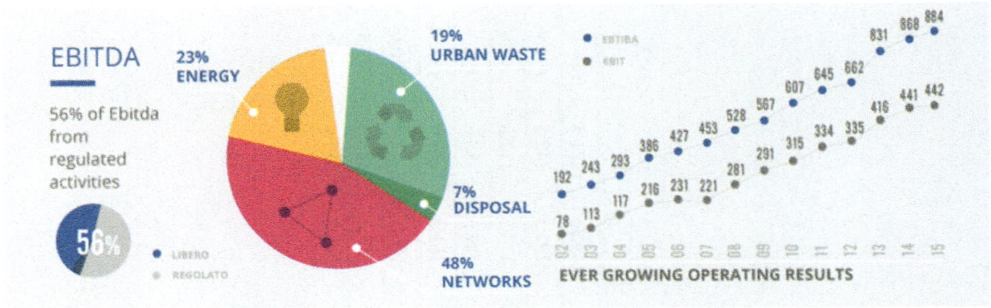

Fig. 4.1 Hera activities and operating results, Hera website, accessed 28 June 2016

Today, Hera with its 8500 employees provides services to about 3.5 million of customers dwelling in 358 municipalities located in thirteen Provinces in the Centre-North-East of the Italian peninsula.

The shareholding structure of the Hera group counts over 118 public shareholders, mainly municipalities in the reference territory, which hold a total of about 51.9 % of the share capital. The shareholder structure is characterized by the presence of numerous municipalities, with a relatively low concentration of shares and a private shareholding spread. At present, the rest of the shares are owned by private investors, 39.9 % of free float and 8.2 % of private shareholder agreements (Hera 2016a). The shareholding structures require Hera to manage a complex situation in which multiple stakeholders, private shareholders, government and local community, have a legitimate claim on accountability over its performances. Considering the fact that Hera provides public services and is owned by private and public stakeholders, there are many benefits that could be gained from adopting integrated reporting. Given the broad shareholder base and the nature of its activities, Hera is subject to several and often conflicting expectations which could be better met through the proper communication tool.

Under the organizational structure point of view, the Hera group has a financial holding at the top of the structure, deliberately created to achieve a more integrated management of the whole group.

4.4 Event History Database: 13 Years Towards Integrated Reporting in Hera

Hera has been committed towards sustainability since 2003. The production of the Sustainability Report has been so pervasive in Hera and has produced a deep impact on the organisation. In particular, the publication of the Sustainability Report has been influential in the organisational structure and in the producing and disclosing process of the information contained in the report, as can be seen in Table 4.4.

From the first point of view a specific organisational structure of Hera has been devoted to the drawing up and the issuing of the Sustainability Report, a Corporate

Table 4.4 CSR timeline since 2003, Sustainability reports of Hera, years (2004, 2005, 2006, 2007, 2008, 2009, 2010, 2011, 2012, 2013, 2014, 2015, 2016a, b); Hera website, accessed 28 June 2016

2016	The Sustainability Report drawn up according to GRI G4
2015	First Risk management policy of the Group
2014	CSR online awards 2014: 2nd place for Hera
	The Risk Committee is appointed by the Board of Directors
	The Board of directors approves the update of the Code of Ethics
2013	Hera obtains SA8000 social certification
2012	More than 100 messages from the public for Hera's Sustainability Report discussed
2011	Hera obtains the OHSAS 18001 workplace safety certification
	The Diversity Manager for the Group is appointed
	The Group presents the Sustainability Report for the first time in all areas: 7 events 1,000 participants
2010	Appointed the Corporate Social Responsibility Division
2009	The 2008 Sustainability Report was audited according to the new standard AA1000 Assurance Standard
	Sustainability Report on line
	Hera signs Charter for equal opportunities and equality in the workplace
2008	The Board of Directors approved the 2007 Sustainability Report for the first time at the same time with Financial Statement
	Sustainability Report presented for the first time to the Shareholders
2007	The Board of Directors approves Sustainability Report
	The Sustainability Report 2006 presented for the first time
	The Sustainability Report drawn up according to GRI G3 (level A+)
	The Board of Directors approved the new Group Code of Ethics and appointed the Ethics Committee
	The commencement of the training course aimed at introducing the Code of Ethics
2006	Balanced Scorecard incentive system, which integrate sustainability aspects, extended to all executives
	The Board of Directors approved the new Mission and Charter of Values
	Hera received ISO 14001 environmental management certification
2005	Hera's plan for Corporate Social Responsibility presented to Board of Directors
	Created the Corporate Social Responsibility Unit
	First annual customer satisfaction survey
	First biennial internal climate survey
2004	Ratified the commitment to the aims of the Global Compact
	Hera received ISO 9001 quality management certification
2003	First Sustainability Report of the Hera Group

Social Responsibility Unit, in a staff position for the Chief Executive Officer in 2005, and the Corporate Social Responsibility Division in 2010. The latter has the aim to ensure that the social responsibility principles are an integral part of the corporate planning and management processes. Specifically, the CSR Department has the objective of drawing up and proposing guidelines for corporate social responsibility, preparing the sustainability report and overseeing the balanced scorecard system. Since 2010, the CSR Department has been structured in three units, namely the BSC System Management, Sustainability Reporting and CSR Projects.

For a better understanding of the case selection and its results, it is opportune to underline the nature of the Sustainability Report of Hera. It is the final result of a process that starts from the stakeholders and finishes by providing them with the integrated information, as the integrating thinking process requires. Hence, despite the name of the Sustainability report, it is correct to speak of an "integrating reporting process", as showed in the report and on the organization website.

The strategic focus feature of an integrated reporting is one of the three most important elements that Eccles et al. (2015) argue to be recognised as of great importance. The authors claim that "there distinguishing marks of a truly integrated report—one that is not simply the outcome of combining two separately conceived and prepared reports: (1) an explanation of a company's strategy for creating value and how it uses and affects the "six capitals" (Financial, Manufactured, Intellectual, Human, Social and relationship, and Natural); (2) a clear and detailed explanation of the relationships between financial and nonfinancial performance; and (3) identification and effective presentation of the material risks and opportunities facing the company" (Eccles et al. 2015: 103).

As written in the 2015 Sustainability Report (pp. 4–5), "Our business strategy embraces sustainability: this is our approach. Our business plan is divided into four strategic lines—growth, excellence, efficiency and innovation. Sustainability, in its various spheres, is cross-cutting through the four lines and has been a key priority for the Group ever since its establishment. Its integration in our business activities is implemented through: strong attention to systems of values, at the basis of our activities, […]; continuous improvement of the Group's accountability profile, as witnessed by the report and by the vertical theme reports which explain in detail what we do and how we do it with regard to particularly sensitive issues […]; a balanced scorecard system associated with a bonus system involving all management and in which sustainability objectives account averagely for 20 % of variable remuneration in 2015; strengthening of the governance system and management of business risks, according to a renewed integrated system for enterprise risk management, managed with a view to maintaining operations and to ensuring safety".

Moreover, and with a specific focus on strategy and sustainability integration, the approach adopted by Hera is based on integrating sustainability in its planning and control systems and therefore, in the management of its business activities. Since 2007 this aspect has been effectively implemented through a balanced scorecard (BSC) system involving all management and with constant commitment to stakeholder reporting, as confirmed by the sustainability report (Fig. 4.2).

Fig. 4.2 Hera's cycle from strategy to daily management, Hera sustainability report (2016b), p. 11

Considering the second mark concerning a clear and detailed explanation of the relationships between financial and non-financial performance, some indicators relative to the sustainability strategy have been included in all the different documents of Hera: the strategic plan, the budget, and BSC, as well as the pay for performance system of managers. This process allows a sound integration of financial and non-financial aspects related to the implementation of the different projects and Hera's sustainability strategy.

The third mark is about the identification and effective presentation of the material risks and opportunities facing the organization. In the overall design of the risk management process, Hera has adopted a risk management practice which aims at defining a systematic approach which is consistent with risk control and management. In this vein, the creation of an effective model with steering, monitoring and representation functions has to be read, oriented towards the adequacy of the management processes and their compliance with the goals of top management.

This approach was established following the approval of the Group's risk management policy by the Board of Directors. The policy defines the Group's orientation with regard to risk issues and identifies the risk management framework defining: "the risk model by identifying the scope of reference for the risk management analysis carried out by the Group; the Group's risk propensity which defines the acceptable risk level in compliance with the risk management strategy, by identifying key risk dimensions, key metrics and associated limits; risk management activities, divided into enterprise risk management […] and ongoing risk management […]" (Hera 2016b: 23). The Risk Committee has a duty to prepare of operational guidelines and specific analysis, for monitoring and controlling the various activities.

The Hera Sustainability Report has not suffered major changes since being drawn up in 2002. The 2016 report, referred to 2015 is the last published and has a structure that is almost similar from previous years. The similarities between reports came from the application of the AA1000 standard that has the aim to guarantee transparency about the effects of sustainability policies, decisions, actions, products and performances, thanks to the stakeholder involvement (Accountability UK 2008). The materiality principle is closely related as well as the extent to which an organization demonstrates to responds to its stakeholders.

4.5 The Gap Analysis: Comparing the Sustainability Report of Hera with the IR Framework

The 2015 Sustainability Report was drawn up on the basis of the AA1000 standard which provides the steps required for preparing social and sustainability reports, as previously stated.

The report content matter was selected in compliance with GRI and GBS guidelines. In this issue of the Report, for the second time running, guidelines GRI-G4 were used as a reference together with the sector supplement dedicated to electric utilities (Electric Utilities Sector Disclosures). The Guidelines GRI-G4 mark a significant change in sustainability reporting since they place the aspects and topics considered "material" for stakeholders at the heart of the process.

The GBS standard is more accounting based (Gruppo Bilancio Sociale 2013), and focuses on the principle for drawing up the social balance sheet. In particular, the standard stresses the necessity to disclose the value added produced by the organisation and its distribution among the different stakeholders.

Lastly, Hera is committed to the aims of the Global Compact since 2004. In 2011, its annual communication on progress achieved, represented by the Sustainability Report, was acknowledged as being an advanced level within the Differentiation Programme launched by Global Compact in the same year.

Coherently with the aforementioned standards, the Hera Sustainability Report is structured in three sections. "The first section of the report describes the company's identity, its mission, corporate strategies, sustainability policies, the key indicators for assessing economic, environmental and social sustainability, the dialogue with stakeholders and the corporate economic returns using the methodology based on value added allocated to stakeholders proposed by the GBS. The next sections provide an account of the results achieved for each class of stakeholder, given as performance ratings of a qualitative and quantitative nature and related to the objectives set forth in the previous report and achievement of these. In each section, the stakeholder listening, dialogue and involvement initiatives are indicated. The objectives for the coming years for each class of stakeholder have been set in line with the company's strategic planning instruments; in certain cases, future targets which the company has committed to have been specified with numeric indicators"

(Hera 2016b, p. 283). The classes of stakeholders in the Hera's Sustainability Report are customers, workforce, shareholders and financial institutions, environment and future generations, and suppliers. The third and last section is the methodological guide to the report.

Having introduced the main features of the Hera's Sustainability Report for 2015, it appears worthwhile to apply the Eccles et al. (2015) model to perform a gap analysis. As explained in the methodology section of this work, the testing of the framework provides results on the adherence of Hera's current reporting system as compared to the IR framework guidelines. The main findings are presented in Table 4.5, which shows a summary of the main estimations resulting from the analysis, separated between guiding principles and content elements of the IR framework.

Firstly, it is possible to notice that the overall result, which is comprised of the adherence level of both guiding principles and content elements, is about 78.7 %. That value represents a medium-to-high level of coherence with the IR requirements. Furthermore, in splitting the two components of coherence to guiding principle and content elements, Hera achieves 72.4 % for the level of coherence to the IR in the guiding principles, and 85.1 % in the content elements. However, there could be a margin for a more concise document. The gap analysis demonstrates that Hera's

Table 4.5 Coherence of Hera's current sustainability reporting to IR

	Coherence to IR (%)
IR guiding principles	
Strategic focus and future orientation	70.0
Connectivity of information	50.0
Stakeholder relationships	100.0
Materiality	40.0
Conciseness	50.0
Reliability and completeness	100.0
Consistency and comparability	100.0
Result	72.4
IR content elements	
Organizational overview and external environment	100.0
Governance	100.0
Business model	70.0
Risks and opportunities	100.0
Strategy and resource allocation	75.0
Performance	60.0
Outlook	85.7
Basis of preparation and presentation	100.0
General reporting guidance	75.0
Result	85.1
Overall result	**78.7**

current reporting system has a high level of disclosure concerning contents and information that should be reported in an integrated reporting.

Overall, it is possible to notice that Hera's Sustainability Reporting has a high level of coherence to principles and elements also required by the application of other standards, for stakeholder relationships, and reliability along with completeness, which are all features strongly related to the GRI4 guidelines. More in general terms, it is possible to draw a connection between the information disclosed and the requirements of certain Sustainability standards. For example, the information required for the content elements Organizational overview and external environment and Governance are all required by the GRI's General Standard Disclosure, the GBS and AA1000.

It could be inferred that the application of some reporting standards and guidelines, such as the GRI4, AA1000 and GBS that share many features with the IR framework, place organizations in a privileged position in order to prepare an integrated report.

In summary, Hera integrated thinking is pervasive in its Sustainability reporting. The actions to be undertaken to achieve all the benefits of IR are the following:

Deeper disclosure on intangibles and their linkage to value creation could be able to better represent and communicate the full value of the intangibles of the group and gain a higher stock price value. Moreover, integrating financial and non-financial information can more effectively explain investments and their linkage to the Hera's value creation processes.

Improved disclosure on long-term strategies and objectives that will overcome the lack of long-term strategies and goals in the annual report as well as on the sustainability report. This action could enable the group to clearly disclose the information and the limit given by information asymmetries, which often cause over or under valuation of organizations.

Increased clarity about relationships and commitments from the management perspective will create the framework and context to increase inter-departmental linkages and understanding of the interrelationships between the different sectors of the organization.

Deepen the engagement with all stakeholders is a highly material benefit. In fact, if stakeholders can have an improved comprehension of the linkages between financial and non-financial activities, there could be a decrease in conflicting expectations from the different stakeholders or at least a better understanding of the organization as a whole.

4.6 Management Accounting Change Process in Hera

To analyse the management accounting change process within Hera, the Armstrong (2006) model has been adopted. The eight steps proposed to enact actions can now be discussed in conjunction with activities that took place in Hera over the 2003 to 2015 period.

The first step is establishing a *sense of urgency*, which originates by taking into consideration the market and competitive realities, and identifying and discussing crises or major opportunities. The introduction of the sustainability report in 2003 and its improvements until 2015, are strongly connected to the commitment of the organization with sustainability. In that vein, the sense of urgency that animated Hera's behaviour derives from the internal need to represent the business sustainability. That is the reason why Hera was a pioneer of sustainability reporting in 2003 as well as a pioneer of integrated thinking in 2016.

Over time the sense of urgency undertook some modifications concerning the directions to take to respond to the pressures, but remained unchanged in its nature, due to the existence of long-term environmental pressures. The external pressures resulted in changes both in the organizational structures (new groups of people for new tasks) and new management accounting systems (new models and metrics for measuring the results of the new activities).

In response to the sense of urgency Hera decided to form a *powerful guiding coalition* by assembling a group with enough power to lead the change effort and encouraging the group to work together as a team. Over time, the guiding collation received increased attention. The availability of key people leading the change was a key element in Hera. At the beginning the Board of Directors and then the Sustainability Reporting Division took responsibility in implementing practical changes at all levels of the organization. Facing the challenge of the sustainability reporting introduced in 2003, in 2005 the Board of Directors decided to create a Social Responsibility Unit specifically devoted to the sustainability effort, as well as to approve a plan for Corporate Social Responsibility. The following year the Board of Directors approved the new Mission and Charter of Values and subsequently in 2007 the new Group Code of Ethics and appointed the Ethics Committee. Then following the expansion of Hera in the region and the complexity arising from the changed features of the business over more than 10 years, in 2010 Hera appointed the Corporate Social Responsibility Division and in 2014 the Diversity Manager and the Risk Committee. The latter in 2015 produced the first Risk Management Policy of Hera. The Board of Directors represents the powerful guiding coalition that acted as the enabler of the integrated thinking over time and establishing many other coalitions to drive the change effort.

Creating a vision to help direct the change effort and in turn developing strategies for achieving that vision, is the third step of the model. Vision and values should be able to inspire and orientate the decision-making process of the organization. Hera's vision is to become 'the best multiutility in Italy for its customers, workforce and shareholders' (Hera website, accessed July 2016). Hera aims to achieve its vision with the development of 'an original corporate model capable of innovation and of forging strong links with the areas in which it operates by respecting the local environment' (Hera website, accessed July 2016).

In the autumn of 2005, the vision and values established in 2002 were reviewed and revised. A work group was set up for this purpose, made up of CSR, Personnel and Organisation, the Bologna Area and the External Relations. The group was entrusted with the task of defining company vision and formulating a proposal for a

Vision and a Charter of Values for consideration by the Executive Committee. The process of vision creation took place also *empowering others* to act on the vision by eliminating obstacles for change, changing systems or structures that seriously undermine the vision and encourage risk taking and non-traditional ideas, activities and actions. The employees of Hera were involved in the process by way of the creation of number of focus groups and the circulation of a questionnaire composed of a quantitative section, whereby values and principles were laid out in the proposal and were rated from 1 to 10, and a qualitative section was presented where participants could express their personal views was shown. Additionally, the mayors of Hera's 15 shareholder municipalities shared their opinions through interviews. 29 % of the employees completed and submitted the questionnaire, expressing their approval of the draft with an average rating around 7.5. The results were incorporated and approved by the Executive Committee and the Board of Directors in June 2006, paving the way for the final draft of the vision, charter of values and working principles.

The described process provided the opportunity to *communicate the vision,* using every vehicle possible, to communicate the new vision and strategies, and teaching new behaviours by the example of the guiding coalition. To that aim, in line with the revision of the organization vision and charter of values, in September 2006 the group began the process of revising its Code of Ethics, approved in 2007. In the same year Hera initiated a training course aimed at introducing the entire corporate body to the company values and principles and rules of the code of Ethics. The classroom training took place until autumn 2008 involving all employees.

Planning for and creating short-term wins, planning for visible performance improvement, creating those improvements and recognizing and rewarding employees involved in the improvements. The involvement of employees, both present and prospective, drove Hera to fourth place in 2011 and first place in 2012 Lundquist Employer Branding 2012 Awards, a kind of Oscar awarded to the best of 100 Italian companies (listed and unlisted) for attractiveness as an employer to potential employees. Essentially, the award recognises the quality of a website section which communicates information on the organization, its vision, the goals that it wishes to achieve within the organisation, and the ways it develops, trains and manages its employees. It represents a clear plan that Hera is seeking to create short-term wins concerning ethical and social responsibility, taking care about the communication of what it means to work at Hera: organisation, business units, opportunities, career paths, compliance with ethical values and corporate social responsibility. And it also represents a publicly available change agenda of the organization's employees.

> It is aimed at conveying – both internally and externally – the values on which the company is founded: the pursuit of excellence, the centrality of individuals, team spirit, and attention to sustainability. We are certain that this not only helps to guide the choices of those who apply for jobs with us, but also strengthens the sense of belonging for all of our existing employees.
>
> General Director of Personnel and Organisation

The following step is *consolidating improvements and producing still more change* by using increased credibility to change systems, structures and polices that do not fit the vision, hiring, promoting and developing employees who can implement the vision and reinvigorating the process with new projects, themes and change agents. Hera realizes a biannual internal climate survey to monitor improvement actions over time. The general strategy is to strive for continuous improvement and innovation within Hera to last and improve society and the environment for future generations. The hot topic of the climate survey is the commitment with social responsibility, as

> We encourage environmental and social responsibility because we believe the environment is a social and economic treasure that must be protected for a sustainable future. Our people are crucial in obtaining our business objectives, so engaging and bringing out the best in them is a priority.
>
> Managing Director

Lastly, *institutionalizing new approaches* possible by articulating the connections between new behaviours and corporate successes, and developing the means to ensure leadership development and succession. The institutionalization process in Hera takes place making use of different actions, enhancing and spreading knowledge of the Group's policies with particular focus on the recently introduced changes; defining actions and procedures to share important information and promoting moments for dialogue between managers and workers, in order to ensure the circulation of information; developing the ability of managers to assign objectives, exercise delegated powers and provide feedback within the development process; strengthening knowledge about the group's corporate social responsibility projects and its results, updating the code of ethics with the involvement of workers. Improving behaviours and increasing knowledge are the key terms that can be used to summarize the path towards the institutionalization of the new approaches in Hera.

To conclude, the emergence of the need for change in Hera and the initial positive reaction of the people involved with change, under a strong coalition guided and supported the progressive adoption of the integrated thinking. Subsequently, for the process to be activated in a positive way there is a need for top management commitment, communication, professional training and support systems developing new behaviours and securing universal participation in the throughout the change process. Key in supporting participants to adjust to the continuously changing environment, is the necessity to keep communication open and to maintain the organization's clear vision throughout the change process. During final stage of the change process, and to make the entire process successful, Hera's new practices are enforced by continuous repetition, evaluation and rewarding in order to be totally institutionalized and lead to the positive outcome of the management accounting change process.

References

Adams CA (2015) The international integrated reporting council: a call to action. Crit Perspect Acc 27:23–28

Armstrong M (2006) A handbook of human resource management practice, 10th edn. Kogan Page, London

Bennett A, Elman C (2006) Qualitative research: recent developments in case study methods. Annu Rev Polit Sci 9:455–476

Brown AD, Jones MR (1998) Doomed to failure: narratives of inevitability and conspiracy in a failed IS project, Organ Stud 19(1)

Eccles RG, Krzus MP (2010) One report. Integrated reporting for a sustainable society. Wiley, USA

Eccles RG, Krzus MP (with Sidney Ribot) (2015a) The integrated reporting movement: meaning, momentum, motives, and materiality. Wiley, New Jersey

Eccles RG, Krzus MP, Ribot S (2015b) Models of best practice in integrated reporting. J Appl Corp Finance 27(2):103–115

Eisenhardt KM (1989) Building theories from case study research. Acad Manage Rev 14(4):532–550

Eisenhardt KM, Graebner ME (2007) Theory building from cases: opportunities and challenges. Acad Manage J 50(1):25–32

Gruppo Bilancio Sociale (2013) Standard GBS 2013—Principi di redazione del bilancio sociale. http://www.gruppobilanciosociale.org/standard-gbs-2013-principi-di-redazione-delbilancio-Sociale. Accessed 28 June 2016

Guba EG, Lincoln YS (2005) Paradigmatic controversies, contradictions, and emerging influences. In: Denzin NK, Lincoln YS (eds) The sage handbook of qualitative research, 3rd edn. Sage Publications, Thousand Oaks, CA, pp 191–215

Hera (2004) Il Bilancio di Sostenibilità (Sustainability report) 2003, not available in English

Hera (2005) Il Bilancio di Sostenibilità (Sustainability report) 2004, not available in English

Hera (2006) Il Bilancio di Sostenibilità (Sustainability report) 2005, not available in English

Hera (2007) Il Bilancio di Sostenibilità (Sustainability report) 2006, not available in English. http://eng.gruppohera.it/group. Section social responsibility. Accessed June 2016

Hera (2008) Il Bilancio di Sostenibilità (Sustainability report) 2007, not available in English. http://eng.gruppohera.it/group. Section social responsibility. Accessed June 2016

Hera (2009) Sustainability report 2008. http://eng.gruppohera.it/group. Section social responsibility. Accessed June 2016

Hera (2010) Sustainability report 2009. http://eng.gruppohera.it/group. Section social responsibility. Accessed June 2016

Hera (2011) Sustainability report 2010. http://eng.gruppohera.it/group. Section social responsibility. Accessed June 2016

Hera (2012) Sustainability report 2011. http://eng.gruppohera.it/group. Section social responsibility. Accessed June 2016

Hera (2013) Sustainability report 2012, http://eng.gruppohera.it/group. Section social responsibility. Accessed June 2016

Hera (2014) Sustainability report 2015. http://eng.gruppohera.it/group. Section social responsibility. Accessed June 2016

Hera (2015) Sustainability report 2014. http://eng.gruppohera.it/group. Section social responsibility. Accessed June 2016

Hera (2016a) Annual report 2015. http://eng.gruppohera.it/group. Section investor relations. Accessed June 2016

Hera (2016b) Sustainability report 2015. http://eng.gruppohera.it/group. Section social responsibility. Accessed June 2016

Higgins C, Stubbs W, Love T (2014) Walking the talk(s): organisational narratives of integrated reporting. Acc Auditing Accountability J 27(7):1090–1119

International Integrated Reporting Committee (IIRC) (2013) Framework for integrated reporting and the integrated report. www.integratedreporting.com. Accessed July 2016

Kotter JP (1996) Leading change. Harvard Business School Press, Boston, MA

Lincoln Y, Guba EG (1985) Naturalistic inquiry. Sage Publications, Newbury Park, CA

Ruggiero P, Mofardini P (2013) The case of Hera. In: Busco C, Frigo ML, Riccaboni A, Quattrone P (eds) Integrated reporting: concepts and cases that redefine corporate accountability. Springer, Switzerland, pp 313–330

Van der Stede WA (2014) A manipulationist view of causality in cross-sectional survey research. Acc Organ Soc 39(7):567–574

Van de Ven AH, Poole MS (2005) Alternative approaches for studying organizational change. Organ Stud 26(9):1377–1404

Yin RK (1989) Case study research: design and methods, rev. edn. Sage Publications, Newbury Park, CA

Yin RK (1994) Case study research—design and methods. Sage Publications, London